'The intricate world of masculinities and fatherhood is explored through the refreshing lens: the eyes of children. Groundbreaking and emotionally resonant, by blending cinematic examples, it offers a transformative perspective building on the complex legacy of masculinity and men's studies. A must-read for understanding intricate gender dynamics in families.'

Professor Simon Macklin, *University for the Creative Arts, UK*

'Holmwood brilliantly explores the intertwining of masculinity studies and psychosocial approaches in this penetrating study of negative father figures and the traumas they inflict on their children. The book simultaneously reminds us of the wounds that absent, abusing or violent fathers cause, but also highlights the children's possibility of renewal and overcoming difficulties. This is a vital contribution to fatherhood studies, grounded in Jungian theories and extensive, original analysis of Hollywood and international films.'

Dr Elena Caoduro, *Queen's University Belfast, UK*

Shadows of Fatherhood, Jung, and Film

Every picture tells a story, and stories have the power to educate. Looking at two key Jungian archetypes – the father and the shadow – from a challenging perspective, this book investigates the negative, shadowy side of fatherhood and its detrimental effect on children by presenting a collection of stories from all over the world.

Blurring the line between fiction and fact, art and academic theory, the book travels across a difficult psychosocial landscape, discussing family life, mental health, and criminality. Mark Holmwood highlights the educational value of these stories while exploring the father–child dynamic, adverse childhood experiences, father hunger, asymmetrical power relations, psychological manipulation, narcissism, domestic violence, sexual abuse, patricide, and filicide. Jungian and post-Jungian viewpoints on the bond between fathers and their children are woven into a bigger, interconnected narrative which invites the readers to re-think clinical, sociological, and mythological connections through the lens of modern masculinity and men's studies. Discussing five different types of negative fathers, the book presents their children's struggles and underlines their resilience at the same time, emphasising assertion, challenge, questioning, and if necessary, acceptance, all being a part of the complex and transformative psychological process called individuation.

Written with a clear and direct style, *Shadows of Fatherhood, Jung, and Film* will be of interest to mental health professionals, Jungian scholars, students, teachers, and researchers in social sciences, humanities, and the arts, as well as general readers with a distinctive interest in men's studies, father–child relations, and cinema.

Mark Holmwood, PhD, is a scholar whose transdisciplinary research focuses on observable patterns of human behaviour. He is the author of *Traumatic Loss and Recovery in Jungian Studies and Cinema*, also published by Routledge.

Shadows of Fatherhood, Jung, and Film

Mark Holmwood

Routledge
Taylor & Francis Group

LONDON AND NEW YORK

Designed cover image: © Getty Images

First published 2025
by Routledge
4 Park Square, Milton Park, Abingdon, Oxon OX14 4RN

and by Routledge
605 Third Avenue, New York, NY 10158

Routledge is an imprint of the Taylor & Francis Group, an informa business

British Library Cataloguing in Publication Data
A catalogue record for this book is available from the British Library

Library of Congress Cataloging-in-Publication Data
Names: Holmwood, Mark, author.
Title: Shadows of fatherhood, Jung, and film / Mark Holmwood.
Description: Abingdon, Oxon ; New York, NY : Routledge, 2025. |
Includes bibliographical references and index. |
Identifiers: LCCN 2024010931 (print) | LCCN 2024010932 (ebook) |
ISBN 9781032495767 (hardback) | ISBN 9781032495743 (paperback) |
ISBN 9781003394488 (ebook)
Subjects: LCSH: Jungian psychology. | Fatherhood--Psychological aspects.
Classification: LCC BF173.J85 H55 2025 (print) | LCC BF173.J85 (ebook) |
DDC 150.19/54--dc23/eng/20240423
LC record available at https://lccn.loc.gov/2024010931
LC ebook record available at https://lccn.loc.gov/2024010932

ISBN: 978-1-032-49576-7 (hbk)
ISBN: 978-1-032-49574-3 (pbk)
ISBN: 978-1-003-39448-8 (ebk)

DOI: 10.4324/9781003394488

Typeset in Times New Roman
by Taylor & Francis Books

To Chris,
for being a better man
than his father ever was

Contents

Acknowledgements

I'll be frank. Writing another book with a heavy – and downright distressing – subject matter, following the one on grief and loss, felt crazy. I'm not particularly referring to the difficulty of writing about family issues which are full of pain, heartache, despair, and, most of the time, isolation. But the topic made many people react first with surprise, concern, and bewilderment. 'Have you lost your mind?' or 'Why don't you give yourself a break and do something else instead?' were among the most typical and frequent lines I heard during the writing of this book. So yes, it was a bit crazy. But then, when we talked about it, these people realised and appreciated the importance of the theme. As the saying goes, home is where the heart is. And if that heart is neglected, broken, abused by parents, fathers, or father figures then that home becomes the black hole of the soul. It goes everywhere, swallows up every bit of joy, and is present in every moment until death. What is expected to be one of the greatest nurturing emotional bonds becomes one of the worst and crippling burdens.

Therefore, this rather taboo perspective on fathers led to many, many, many hours of discussion, reminiscing, analysis of the past and the present, including individuals as well as social structures and cultures, triggering laughter and tears. I would like to thank Amy Murphy, Freja Kamann, Eelin Hokkanen, Avi Fisher, Keiji Hayakawa, Julio Placido, Nermin Aksu, Nezih Tanrıöver, Theo Stavropoulos, Annelies Joosten, David Morales, Mehar Chandra-Moore, and Adwin Achebe for their insight, comments, and encouragement. Many thanks to David Thompson for chocolate support, Kim Sue Palm for exceptional and unexpected culinary escapades, and Mary and Arthur Bailey for their family wisdom. Special thanks to a special group of counsellor friends – Nathaniel Steiner, Jim Davis, Bella Clifton, Lewis Cooper, Peter Dragiewicz, and Hanna Virtanen. You have light, you bring light, you protect light.

I am grateful to the University of Sussex and the university library staff for their generosity and assistance during the research and writing of this book.

Last but not least, many thanks to Katie Randall, Manon Berset, and Kris Šiošytė at Taylor & Francis, and to Hamish Ironside, for their interest, swift, kind and diligent solutions during the publication process. It's been a pleasure – again – to work with you.

Introduction

Yes, it is one of the most recurring, simple, and iconic scenes in many films. It sometimes looks like it was copied and pasted from another film. It gets recreated in many, many different formats because it is taken directly from real life. You know that scene very well. You have seen it many times. Even better, you have experienced it yourself. Your father reads you a bedtime story.

The scene takes place in a familiar, soft, homely setting. The child is tucked up, comfy and warm in their bed. Towards the corner of the bed, there is a plush toy, or maybe a doll. The father lies down next to the child, with a book in hand. The lighting of the room is soft. Maybe there are little glowing stars and planets on the wall, making the scene even more magical. Slowly and gently, the father reads. The child listens. Not a word the father says is missed. There is an unwavering attention. And really, it does not matter if the story is read for the tenth time or not. It truly does not matter if the child knows every word by heart. It is the comfort and the safety that matters. Feeling, knowing there is no harm or danger, the child slowly relaxes into the night, listening to the voice of the father.

The bedtime story can be funny, uplifting, hopeful, or downright scary. If it is the former, the joy and the fun of the story transcend its paper limits and instil a sense of optimism in the child, shared with the father. If it is a ghost story, for example, the cosy and the sheltered space at home acts as an invisible shield for the child. Plus, there is the presence of the father. As a parent, he can and will protect the child from ghosts, vicious ghouls, and terrifying monsters. He will make sure that the child wakes up in the morning, unharmed and without a scratch, having learned a bit more about the distinction between fantasy and reality.

This book explores this distinction and, in many parts, deliberately blurs the line between fact and fiction. In more ways than one, it is a story book for adults about fathers and fatherhood. It explores the dark, shadowy, destructive, and sometimes terrifying aspects of being a parent and how these character traits affect children. Through expanding and amplifying the metaphors and storylines in different films, it examines the damaging actions and choices of different fathers and how these actions ripple in time throughout the lives of their children. By comparing and contrasting them with similar and sometimes different case studies, the fictional relationships between negative fathers and their children become unique vignettes to discuss the factual damage children face in their youth which they can carry into their adult future.

The first question that comes to mind might be 'why'. Does the world need another book focused on parenthood? Better yet, does the world need a negative father book? In fact, the market is saturated with parenting books, all guiding people, encouraging them to do more, to do better, to become an exemplary, perhaps enviable parent. A quick search on Amazon, for example, with the word 'parenting', brings over 60,000 book results. If you take the same search to Google Books, it brings you 'about 6,180,000 results' (at the time of writing). These overwhelming numbers indicate that there is a plethora of information, guidance, and opinion on how to be a good (or better) parent, how to navigate through challenging situations with children, or simply how to ignore the experts when it comes to parent–child relationships.

This information overload continues when you modify the search parameter and include 'father' as the keyword. Under the 'Parenting and Relationships' category, Amazon, again, brings over 60,000 results, covering topics such as fertility, adoption, marriage, childcare, and even aging parents. From guides for soon-to-be fathers (Brott and Rudick, 2021) to the physical and psychological challenges of primary caregivers (Boss, 2011), from transforming parent–child relationships into mature and loving connections (Newman, 2003) to dealing with PTSD as a result of having a narcissistic father (Foster, 2020), the vast landscape of the bond between a father and a child is explored in many and inventive ways covering both clinical and personal settings.

It is, of course, impossible to cover all these perspectives in one book; historical, religious, sociological and at times deeply psychoanalytical viewpoints provide different pieces of a growing and evolving puzzle, trying to dissect and analyse an idea and hopefully come up with a more coherent way of looking at it. This idea, or rather the question is simple: what is a father? The Oxford English Dictionary goes to the root of the word 'father' and highlights an Indo-European origin, shared by Greek (*patēr*) and Latin (*pater*), from which the Old English (*fæder*) and Germanic derivatives (*vader/vater*) come from. Historically speaking, based on the myths of Ouranos (who was the personification of sky and a primordial deity, son and husband of Gaia, Mother Earth) and then later on Zeus (of which the word 'Deus' is thought to be cognate), a father is a male deity, animal, or human generator of offspring. This power of causing pregnancy resulting in the birth of a progeny, and therefore creating a chain of posterity, became the bedrock of many religions which shaped and strengthened all the cultural associations related to a man.

These associations are still very much reflected in linguistic terms. Apart from being the first person of the Trinity in Christian belief (Heavenly Father), the word father is also used to address a priest. Ancestors are frequently described as forefathers. Again, based on the power of producing offspring, a father is also considered a strong male figure who also provides for and protects his children and descendants. The oldest or the founding members of a society, or important male figures in the origin of something are usually called fathers. These literary and cultural interconnections continue to highlight not only the power of generating children or a valuable idea/product, but also the ability and the capacity to guard, take charge of, and be responsible for the welfare of this offspring.

The birth of language separated humans from other forms of life for good. This differentiation seems to have led to the emergence of all kinds and varieties of opposites in human thinking: reality–illusion; body–spirit; mortality–immortality; animate–inanimate; life–death; and of course, man–woman. Therefore, deities in many parts of the world evolved from animal forms into human forms. The ancient civilisations revered objects in the sky and, even though there was a polytheistic culture, the Moon had a special place within many civilisations as it provided the much-needed light during dark nights. The Moon was a female deity, and the changes of lunar phases, powers of birthing, regeneration, and nourishment coupled with a distinct matriarchal aspect was a shared component observed in the myths of Ishtar, Asherah, Astarte, Isis, Cybele, Diana, Artemis, Hecate, and Juno Lucina. With the arrival/rise of Yahweh, the shift from a woman-centric culture to a patriarchal society went hand in hand with a strong male domination of the world where the Sun god ruled over the Moon goddess. As polytheistic cultures were reorganised into monotheistic ones, the power of creating children now belonged to men.

Scott (1966) notes that the earliest human understanding of sex was indeterminate. In other words, it was androgynous. Male and female were in the same body, combining the powers of creation in a harmonious unity. As the human thinking evolved and separated the two, the responsibility for reproduction was mainly placed on the male. Avoiding marriage, and therefore the purpose and the natural consequence of sexual intercourse, became forbidden. The divine instruction to be fruitful and multiply is repeated several times through the Old Testament. Man, as a direct creation of God and who is given the right to rule over the land, animals, and women, appeared to be destined to be a father, a generational responsibility passed down to each and every male child.

This shift from a matriarchal society to a patriarchal one went hand in hand with what Scott (ibid.) argues as the worshipping of the phallus. Kipinis's (1991) research broadly overlaps with this perspective, especially in his descriptions of the 'Earth Bull Father' observed in the ancient Mediterranean region. This father figure points out a central male individual who acts as an intermediary between the spirit world and the tribe, in other words a shaman who can access and influence supernatural powers and bring divination and healing to the Earthly domain. Several wall paintings of this male figure include depictions of him adorned with bulls' horns and a big erection. Anthropologically speaking, the glorification of the penis, male virility, potency, and strength in creating offspring was also present outside this geographical region in different cultures and belief systems. For example, Gudimallam Lingam in Hinduism, Yang in Chinese philosophy, Kunado and Sahe no Kami in Japanese Shinto all represented a divine, active, and superior male principle impregnating and in direct connection with a receptive and earthly female principle.

Judeo-Christian doctrine suppressed the phallus admiration/imagery of other and earlier belief systems, strengthened man's central position within society, and also presented a Heavenly Father (especially in the Torah) who promises protection and prosperity to his children if they follow his commands (Greenstein, 1983; Abramovitch, 1997). Trepp (1973) argues that Abraham was ultimately looking for an ethical God, different to the ones in ancient Mesopotamia and Greece who, in different ways, were whimsical. They influenced and took advantage of humans based on their selfish motivations. God described in the Hebrew Scriptures, however, clearly sets boundaries, rules, and consequences for disobedience, depicting a mix of a stern but compassionate fatherly behaviour.

While diverse cultures had different varieties of male–female dynamics, the role and the responsibilities of men in a predominantly patriarchal society gradually solidified into three distinct and almost globally accepted categories: procreator; provider; and protector (Levant, 2011). These three principles became a crucial (if not standard) set of norms and expectations that shaped male thinking and behaviour in cultures and communities around the world, not to mention the areas where Abrahamic religions were most influential. Levant and Richmond (2007), when they defined masculinity ideology, pointed out how cultural attitudes and belief systems are ultimately internalised by individuals. This internalisation, they argue, then leads to strict and sometimes inflexible patterns of behaviour in order to comply with society's expectations of boys and men.

Even though masculine traits and standards, such as being confident, gallant, determined, independent, dominant, and commanding (all of which share the same underlying theme of power), can be observed in people regardless of their biological sex, the notion of fatherhood almost always goes hand in hand with the complex concept of manliness, male identity, and masculinity. Gilmore (1990) and Vandello et al. (2008) argue that women attain womanhood via natural and biological developments (such as menstruation, pregnancy, etc.) when they transition from being an adolescent to an adult. The same is partially true for men, too. With the hormonal and biological changes during adolescence, boys gain the capacity to create offspring, one unshakable and universal pillar of manhood. However, men's rites of passage into manhood also include tasks which boys must directly and actively engage with and successfully complete in public. These tasks vary from hunting and killing (Thomas, 1959) to circumcision rituals (Saitoti, 1986) and fraternity ceremonies (Vandello et al., 2008). As these tasks require the public display of personal strength and resolve, however, the status of manhood then becomes a demonstration which is forever tied to the theme of power, an identity which requires proof and regular displays of achievement (such as influence, status, wealth etc.) (Kimmel, 2012; O'Neil, 2015). In other words, manhood might be achieved (and proven), but it is not forever secure as it can be challenged and lost in different ways which troubles lots of men (Vandello et al., 2008). Fatherhood, in this context, becomes intricately entwined with similar expectations and requirements embedded in patriarchal cultures.

Academic research in contemporary Western society has shown that there is a strong link between men's health and the way they follow masculine norms. In particular, the pressure to prove masculinity by displaying traditionally accepted masculine behaviours can affect men's mental health negatively. Pleck (1995) argues that these behaviours include: avoiding any action or mannerism that can be interpreted as feminine; verbal and physical aggression; and self-sufficiency. Generally referred to as the 'dysfunction strain paradigm', this theoretical model is one of two prominent perspectives that look at the relation between masculinity and depression, exploring how masculine norms can become impossible to adhere to (in other words, dysfunctional) and how these situations can burden men's psyche further and trigger depressive symptoms (Rice, Fallon and Bambling, 2011; O'Neil, 2012).

The second theoretical model known as the 'gender norm conformity' presents a more balanced perspective as it documents both the positive and the negative outcomes of adhering to masculine conventions. Developed by Mahalik et al. (2003), the Conformity to Masculine Norms Inventory-94 (CMNI-94) is a psychometric evaluation of the benefits and drawbacks of masculine conformity/nonconformity over 94 different items and 11 major factors. These factors are: winning; emotional control; risk-taking; violence; dominance; playboy; self-reliance; primacy of work; power over women; disdain for homosexuals; and pursuit of status. Abridged later by Parent and Moradi (2009) and Hsu and Iwamoto (2014), this inventory shows that conforming to winning (or having the drive to win), exercising or socialising with friends may protect men from depressive episodes, whereas exaggerated self-reliance which can lead to avoidance in seeking psychological help, or homophobic attitudes (or constant heterosexual self-presentation) may result in poor mental-health, affecting many, if not all interpersonal relationships (Wong et al., 2017).

Sussman (2012), in his book on masculinity, charts the shifting of perspectives throughout history. For example, in Ancient Greece sexual desire and acts between men (to be precise, between adolescent boys and men) were considered a valid social standard of manliness. Serving the king and state as an honourable, devoted warrior or a public servant was another convention. With the arrival of industrial revolution and manufacturing boom in Europe and in America towards the end of the eighteenth century, the power and the wealth of the agriculture dependant hereditary aristocracy started to shift to tradesmen and factory owners. Military bravery or public service no longer defined the identities of this newly emerging economic man. Manliness was displayed and proven via monetary gain, as a financial success story highlighting personal ambition, risk taking, and hard work. The display of this triumph and prosperity was sometimes embellished with a religious attitude as well, proving how faith in God can help men achieve the power and dominance they were destined to have.

The deadliest and widespread conflicts of the First and Second World Wars challenged and altered many aspects of masculinity. The norms men adhered to during peacetime were (re)adjusted to battlefields, and the noble warrior spirit of Ancient Greece found its reincarnation once more. Fatherhood, too, was influenced by this social upheaval, and the desire to restore a more traditional patriarchal identity increased. Especially impacted by the Great Depression when many fathers had to deal with unemployment and lack of money, they were forced to take up a more domestic role which brought resentment and feelings of emasculation. As Elizabeth and Joseph Pleck note, fathers' main goal was money, not paternal involvement (Pleck and Pleck, 1997). Following the wars, as the earning potential of women slowly increased, men felt threatened by this power shift at home. This tricky relationship between gender and labour division where paid work was considered masculine whereas unpaid labour at home as feminine (Holter, 2005; Coontz, 1992, 2005; Cowan, 1983), became one of the prominent theoretical paradigms of feminist social theory.

Women's involvement in and contribution to the paid labour force challenged not only them but also men. Referred to as 'sex segregation' by Charles and Grusky (2004), there are still strong and historically enduring cultural assumptions on the types of jobs that are somehow more appropriate for women (like nursing and being a librarian), and others more appropriate for men (like computer programming or construction) (Wade and Ferree, 2018). Interviews by Williams (1995) show that while male librarians can be mocked for doing a 'woman's job', their career progression is faster compared to female librarians, whereas 'masculinity contest culture' (Berdahl et al., 2018), which is basically a set of highly praised and encouraged behaviours to outperform co-workers and rivals, and which requires men to take risks and dominate others, damages both men and women in workplaces.

Historically speaking, it is important to note that the first wave of feminism did not directly address the notion of masculinity. Even though it challenged and changed the male oriented society (especially on coverture) during the late nineteenth and the early twentieth centuries, the main focus was on women's suffrage and political equality. This first wave's prominent figures, such as Susan B. Anthony, Elizabeth Cady Stanton, and Margaret Fuller in the United States, Barbara Bodichon, Emmeline Pankhurst, and Marie Stopes in the United Kingdom, were successful in raising public awareness and creating the necessary social momentum to achieve gender equality. The

19th Amendment to the US Constitution granting women the right to vote in 1920, and the Representation of the People Act 1918 in the UK were two major electoral and social reforms that broadly coincided with similar developments in Europe and beyond.

While subjects like the marital exemption in rape laws, reproductive rights of women, domestic violence and workplace discrimination were voiced and discussed during the first wave, they were more openly and widely discussed during the second wave of feminism which began in the 1960s and continued into the 1980s. Fuelled by de Beauvoir's (1953) *The Second Sex* (which was banned by the Vatican), Friedan's (1963) *The Feminine Mystique*, and Greer's (1970) *The Female Eunuch*, the movement also saw the emergence of feminist theory which aimed to recognise, challenge and – wherever possible – change the ways in which gender, race, and class intersected to create oppressive structures. Kimberlé Crenshaw's (2017) 'intersectionality' notion provided a new momentum to the third wave feminists in the 1990s as they continued to confront and protest societal norms and stereotypes. This wave of feminism also saw the emergence of the 'riot grrrl' movement, which encouraged and empowered young women via punk rock music and DIY culture, underpinning self-sufficiency, and individuality.

The fourth and the current wave of feminism began in the 2010s and enhances the previous three as well as public awareness. Especially through online activism and the #MeToo movement, the objectification of women and the pervasiveness of sexual harassment and abuse in society (especially in the workplace) were exposed as several women came forward and publicly named and accused the perpetrators. The notion of male privilege (van der Gaag, 2014), and global concerns such as poverty, environmental decay, economic growth, and sustainability are also within the agenda of this wave (Phillips and Cree, 2014). In addition, the fourth wave feminists started the 'SlutWalk' movement to end rape culture (such as victim blaming, slut-shaming or simply trivialising or denying the harm of sexual violence) and raise awareness for sexual consent.

One of the important results of feminist theory is the emergence of masculinity studies (Craig, 1992; Emig and Rowland, 2010). This is due to the critical examination of masculinity and reframing women's roles within changing and evolving social norms, positioning women against the male dominant force which shaped family values, workplace rules and public expectations. This (r)evolution in understanding and questioning gendered assumptions brought on board many men who stood side by side with women, criticising the deeply entrenched sexism and patriarchy in society. Therefore, it is safe to say that this radical shift in awareness became the core of masculinity studies, also known as men's studies, which started to emerge in the 1970s as a response to the second wave of feminism. The field has grown to encompass a wide range of topics, including the social construction of masculinity, men's health and wellness, and the ways in which masculinity intersects with other forms of identity, such as race and sexuality.

   While it is not possible to condense the full scope of men's studies into a paragraph, it is important to mention its three overlapping areas of academic exploration. As Breu (2022) notes, one version of masculinity studies developed parallel to the duality of male and female, and presented a historical timeline of social and cultural phenomena that still shape and constantly change the ideas on what a man is, showing that gender is flexible. Another group of academics collaborated explicitly with feminists to criticise and deconstruct patriarchy, male privilege over femininity, violent and subjugating maleness that permeates notions on religion, race, class and sexuality. The third group of scholarly inquiry brought about a plurality of perspectives on masculinity, including Black, Latin, disabled, queer and trans masculinities, expanding the discussion on power, ideology, gender, hierarchy, and identity. It is also important to note that the types of masculinity politics that shape social trends and alliances identified by Clatterbaugh (1990) are still potent. These are: pro-feminist men; men arguing they are defeated or disadvantaged by feminism; traditionalist and conservative men who insist on standard and customary models of masculinity; mythopoetic men aiming for spiritual development; and men (a combination of left-wing, liberal, gay, and Black groups) who draw attention to the inequalities between men.

   The vast variation among fathers, the intricacy of fathering, and the complexity of the notion of fatherhood have all been heavily researched and debated topics both in psychology and sociology. In more ways than one, it is not possible to detach these topics from the duality of masculinity and feminist studies. Before the emergence of these studies, Talcott Parsons presented his structural functionalism theory, in which he argued that social organisation develops out of social evolution to benefit social cohesion. In doing so, his theory compressed abstract notions into strict institutional practices. Family, as a basic unit, had two essential structures: a generational hierarchy; and two different socialising figures from which the children learn – an instrumental father (a dominant, task-oriented, authority and discipline providing leader) and an expressive mother (a nurturing, emotionally supportive figure, responsible for the well-being of the family) (Parsons, 1949). The functionalist view lost its appeal in sociological thought later on, and feminist thinkers in the 1970s and 1980s revived the discussion on the family in connection with capitalist thinking, especially in terms of gendered division of labour and unpaid housework at home. However, especially in the US, Popenoe (1998) echoed functionalist thinking when he argued that fathers' contribution to the family is mainly financial, and men are not as biologically committed or as attuned as women to be a parent. He also pointed out the promiscuity of men and how this might lead to irresponsible paternal behaviour if there is not enough social and state regulation.

   After Morgan's (1996) influential book *Family Connections*, in which he argued that 'family' is only a set of unfixed, interlinked, and fluctuating relationships (meaning, connections) which change over time, sociological literature has expanded, investigating generational issues, how family relationships overlap with socio-economic practices, and intimacy. Morgan certainly highlighted the importance of individuals and their impact on the formation of cultural and historical values as well as structures, and by speaking of this link between the evolving individual and social order he contributed to Giddens's theory of reflexive process (Giddens, 1992).

At the core of Giddens's argument lies the individual, in other words, the self. He noted that the self is not a fixed entity but an evolving inner narrative, a process which is very much tied to the context of modern life and changing social order, and which unavoidably mirrors these changes in order to generate validity and worth in a way that is meaningful for the individual. Intimacy, he argued, requires mutual and equal disclosure between adults, and when this intimacy is achieved, it transforms the relationships, makes them more democratic, and the results of this transformation would be reflected in the public sphere too. Parents, in this context, must make sure that their children learn discipline and respect in a way that does not ruin the children's individuality.

Research on fathers, contemporary fatherhood, and how these topics overlap with a broader discussion on masculinity (and feminism) is still growing. Some of the more nuanced and cross-cultural empirical investigations include: fathers' long working hours and how this affects their quality time with their children (O'Brien and Shemilt, 2003; Dermott, 2008); discussing whether financial support provided by fathers is already a form of care (Gatrell, 2007); how single fathers do not identify themselves as mothers or a mothering substitute (Doucet, 2006); Black and ethnic minority fathers (Featherstone and White, 2006); fathering experiences of disabled men (Kilkey and Clarke, 2010); and migrant fathers (Kilkey et al, 2014). Apart from these investigations, scholars have also debated hegemonic masculinity (Carrigan et al., 1985; Connell, 1995; Featherstone et al., 2007), meaning how male-dominated institutions sustain, generate, reinforce, and legitimise male power. As Hearn (2002) notes, the notion of patriarchy does not refer to the rule of fathers or the father concept in general anymore. Rather, it highlights the domination of men in social, economic, and political spheres. Therefore, he invites other academics to discuss fatherhood further within the contexts of gender and power.

Especially in the early studies, there seemed to be a habit of making broad generalisations on men and fathers or offering simplified reasons and justifications for complex and multifaceted issues regarding them. Out of this habit emerged a pattern of thinking where the roles of fathers in the past were either depicted better or more appealingly than they really were, or simply portrayed as wicked and corrupt. It is possible to see the echoes of this peculiar absolutist thinking in today's western society where there are incompatible and contradictory ideals for men. As Sussman (2012) notes, men are expected to be assertive, bold, combative, rational, and unsentimental at work and in business, and yet at the same time they are expected to be tender, sensitive, kind-hearted, and compassionate at home as a father and lover. This rather Dr Jekyll and Mr Hyde state of affairs, of course, has also been the focus of psychology and psychoanalysis.

It is important to remember that it was not until the mid-twentieth century that the psychological role and influence of fathers began to be investigated in detail. Social learning theory was the dominant concept in understanding the concept of fatherhood in the 1950s and 1960s. Fathers were responsible for shaping their children's behaviour through being a role model and a source of reinforcement. The critical interventions of feminist scholars, analysing the traditional role of fathers in child development and arguing that fathers' absence or emotional distance having negative consequences for both children and mothers, altered research paradigms and led to many psychologists and attachment theorists increasingly focusing on the importance of involved and nurturing fathers. While it is difficult to pinpoint a definite starting point in history for studies on fatherhood, it is beyond doubt that Freud became one of the most enduring and influential names in understanding family dynamics and father–child relationships.

When Freud turned masculinity into a psychoanalytic inquiry, especially with his takes on father–son rivalry/Oedipal conflicts and the fear of castration, he opened lots of doors for his followers and other thinkers to investigate not only the emotional growth of children but also the political debates and disagreements which fuelled feminism and men's studies. Frosh (1997) argues that Freud saw psychoanalysis as an intellectual and rationalist body of thought, a triumph of mind/reason over senses/emotions. When Freud (1939) specifically positioned fatherhood and motherhood in this dualist thinking, he coined father(hood) with intellectuality and mother(hood) with sensuality, then reframed the Sky-god and Earth-mother relationship in a family context. But he also frequently dealt with the father as a threat to the child, a negative psychoanalytical perspective which has shifted to a more positive one over the years. Especially after the world wars, female psychoanalysts like Klein and Mahler focused on the mother–child relationship which led to the emergence of new theories, such as Winnicott's (1967) *mirroring* concept and Bowlby's (1958) widely influential attachment theory. With Lacan, Freud's Oedipus complex and the importance of the father made an interesting comeback. Lacan's structural linguistic approach was an attempt to decode the language of the unconscious where the (symbolic) father was the imaginary phallus, the lacking element in both the mother's and the child's desires. Historically speaking, it is important to note that while psychoanalytical theory of this period was discussing sexual desire and how it affects parent–child relationships, Harlow's (1958) experiments with rhesus monkeys in the US were contributing to ethology and the main body of attachment theory, demonstrating that motherly love was not sexual.

Attachment theory attracted a lot of criticism as well as support. The way children form (or not form) meaningful, secure, and loving bonds/attachments and how these secure (or insecure) attachments affect patterns of relationship behaviour in their future adult lives became an important discussion and focus of research in psychology and developmental psychology. Parallel to the growing influence of attachment theory, earlier theoretical assumptions based on biological sex gradually adopted environmental influences and developments as well. Researchers began to examine the role of fathers in a wide range of areas in child development, such as how fathers affect mental health and assist positive outcomes in children, how fathers contribute to children's emotional regulation, and the beneficial influence of fathers who treat their partners with respect and equality. The links between the absence of male role models and divorce (Lamb, 1997), father involvement in child upbringing (O'Brien, 2005), and fathers' openness to adopt new perspectives in parenting within the evolving landscape and definitions of masculinity/fatherhood (Henwood and Procter, 2003) are also a few thought-provoking examples of academic exploration. The rise of single-parent families, same-sex parenting, and co-parenting arrangements in contemporary society continue to challenge traditional notions of fatherhood and trigger a greater diversity in scholarly engagement.

Being both a colleague and a rival of Freud, Jung wrote about the importance of fathers, and the role they played in individuals' lives too. Jung's complex theory and list of archetypes – universal and primordial images/ motifs of people, characters, or patterns of behaviour – included two specific figures for parents: father and mother. As the fruit of their union of opposites (in marriage, for example), a child emerged. Through four different case studies, Jung specifically described in the fourth volume of his *Collected Works* (hereafter 'CW') how fathers played a significant role in the destiny of individuals. By specifically using the word 'destiny', he highlighted how both the good and the bad elements of the father–child relationship early in life might become inescapable for adults as they grow up. He noted that father's character had a greater psychological influence on the family, and certainly the child, and this influence could reverberate for centuries due to heredity.

The experience of the father, Jung argued, influenced men and women in different ways. Combining religious elements with human interactions, Jung wrote that father was an 'informing spirit' (CW 5, para. 70), representing spirituality and corresponding to the 'Heavenly Father'. He argued that a positive father complex in men led to a tendency to be too ready to believe that all spiritual dogmas and values are real or true (CW 9i, para. 396) and contributed to their submission to authority. Women, on the other hand, are helped by their father in a different way. Jung wrote that fathers increased women's intellectuality, their *Logos* (CW 5, para. 272), and they instilled a sense of boundary/prohibition as well as wisdom (CW 9i, para. 396). By modern standards (academic and social), these views can cause offence and easily be interpreted as condescending, unprogressive, or sexist. This politically charged discussion, however, is beyond the scope of this book.

Post-Jungian scholars took up the baton on this prickly topic employing different viewpoints to analyse the father–child relationship in detail. For example, Colman and Colman (1998) looked at its mythological connections between the sky and the Earth, and how the role of the father evolved over time. While Corneau (1991) focused on feelings of fatherlessness in males, Jacoby (1999) discussed the place of Jungian psychotherapy in contemporary infant research. From balancing masculinity both with spirituality and contemporary socio-political developments (Tacey, 1997), to healing deeply psychological wounds inflicted by fathers (Gurian, 1992; Hollis, 1994; Schwartz, 2020), academic engagements with the father archetype and the notion of father and fatherhood continued to be fruitful and innovative after Jung.

One of the most recent and comprehensive Jungian perspectives on the father archetype is offered by Weiner and Gallo-Silver (2019). They bring together several core archetypes of Jung, such as the trickster, the mother, and the wounded healer, and combine their fundamental characteristics under five distinct categories which define all the positive and aspirational qualities of fatherhood. Their main argument is that, at any given moment within family life the key to fathering is to achieve a balanced position (similar to balanced nutrition), a sensible, healthy, fair, and varied set of parental behaviour which combines at least two archetypes at any given moment.

Each one of Weiner and Gallo-Silver's categories illustrates and is instrumental in men's fathering potential and capabilities. The *captain* archetype highlights the notion of leadership. Setting rules, boundaries, sticking to clearly established principles, fulfilling duties, anticipating problems, and solving them when necessary are all listed within the definition of this archetype. Proactive planning, ethical and fair assessment, displaying power and control without being high-handed or despotic, qualities which lay the foundations of positive and successful rulers form the core of this fathering style. The flip side of this archetype brings authoritarianism, physical punishment/abuse, or glorification of power and masculinity.

The *educator* archetype is firmly rooted in Jung's wise old man. This type of father revels in communicating knowledge and passing it on to younger generations. In other words, he is the perceptive, insightful, unpretentious guide. He shares his wisdom, illuminates the way for others, helps them understand the world and themselves, all of which pave the way for empowerment and a meaningful life. The educator's shadow becomes the shaming, pompous, hyper-critical father who not only derails the learning process but also alienates the child by being impossible to satisfy. The *protector* archetype, on the other hand, mainly goes parallel to Jung's hero archetype. Providing safety and security for the vulnerable as well as overcoming danger when necessary, a protecting father supports the notions of human connection and empathy through his actions. He keeps his children physically and emotionally safe while helping them thrive as individuals who are free to determine their own lives. The shadow of the protector gives way to either overprotective, paranoid, and continuously suspicious parenting which creates anxious and isolated children who lack necessary social skills to relate to others and are unable to form meaningful bonds, or under-protective parenting which contribute to feelings of abandonment in children especially when they feel their fathers are not present or accessible during stressful or dangerous situations.

The *nurturer* archetype embodies a set of notions which Jung mainly assigns to the mother archetype – love, affection, compassion, and provision of sustenance, in other words nourishment. This archetype is a typical example of a positive father who nourishes his child not only with food but also with warm approval, well-balanced and sensible encouragement, and of course with care and support which is promptly and unconditionally available when the child needs it. The negative side of the nurturer is split into polar opposites – the nurturing father either overwhelms his child with care (aka smothering) or completely denies the child his care, and therefore rejects any involvement. This parental rejection leads to feelings of unworthiness in children, and they grow up with crippling self-esteem issues, thinking they do not deserve to be loved or happy.

The final fatherhood category of Weiner and Gallo-Silver is the *jester* archetype, which borrows most of its qualities from Jung's trickster. Bringing together the playfulness, light-heartedness, mirth, and imagination, fathers who incorporate the jester support the positive outcomes of play – helping their children discover limits, gain physical, mental, and emotional confidence, get rid of excessive energy, or simply relax. This parental perspective also allows children to express their playful misbehaviour without causing harm or serious trouble which contributes to their cognitive processes and understanding of ethics. Just like the nurturer, the jester's negativity manifests in two different opposites. Fathers who exhibit Peter Pan-like behaviour relentlessly undermine or dismiss rules (household or other) in order to be adored by their children, symbolically whisking the child off to a fun-filled universe where limits, responsibilities or promises do not matter. On the other end of this archetype's shadow spectrum lies the father who is always serious and has no interest or desire for play, no time for any joyful activity that is necessary for his child's development. In other words, fathers providing too much, or not enough play might contribute to hedonistic or unreasonably critical/perfectionist behaviour and character in children which are both out of step with reality.

Jung, being very much aware of evil present and embedded in human nature, defined the shadow archetype as the secret inner figure, a hidden, private part of personality where anything immoral, heinous, shocking, or degenerate dwelled. It is the negative total of each and every pleasant, rational, and virtuous quality that is found and observed in man. In Jung's own words, everybody has a shadow (CW 11, para. 131), therefore it is a part of everyone's character. The more this darkness is repressed or denied by the individual, the blacker it gets – meaning, its strength, density, and influence on the consciousness grows, and it (symbolically) becomes a nasty inner twin who would do anything to frustrate the good intentions and deeds of the individual only because it desires to be acknowledged. Simply and eloquently put by Wilmer (1987), shadow is cruelty, intense and selfish desires, ethically wrong impulses, and actions. Above all, it is humanity's unquenchable thirst for power. Power of any and every kind. Power over anything, anyone, everything, and everyone. Power over the past, the present, and the future.

Shadow has many qualities, layers, and as it is unique to each person, it also has countless types. When it comes to fathers and fatherhood, Weiner and Gallo-Silver's examples of shadow open the door to further observation and categorisation. This book goes through that door and follows that perilous path deeper into the darkness which exists in every human being, in every father. As Mullender et al. (2002, p. 178) noted, men's studies – including the ones on fatherhood – have a tendency to shy away from investigating patriarchy, its oppressive and authoritarian orientation, or partner/child abuse even when they examine the negative characteristics of fathering. Therefore, this dark collection of stories, including both fictional and autobiographical examples, explores the negative father without being shy, shining a light on the wounds they inflict on their children.

Chapter 1 looks at the absent father phenomenon. I use James Gray's pensive sci-fi film *Ad Astra* (2019) to investigate the frayed bonds between a (now adult) son and his father who left his family willingly and without remorse many years ago. After exploring the visual clues included in the narrative set in the Solar System, the analysis dives into several aspects of child neglect (Felitti et al., 1998), incorporating academic perspectives on adverse childhood experiences, as well as narcissism (Miller et al., 2011). This chapter also brings the Jungian concepts of persona and individuation into the discussion of father hunger, half-alive children, and inner-regeneration routes for lost sons who are forever hurt by their absent fathers, highlighting the theories of Hollis and Corneau.

In Chapter 2, I dissect Ariel Kleiman's harrowing 2015 film *Partisan* (2015) to unearth the harm a lying, manipulating father can cause. Looking at the real-life criminal underworld of Colombia and how children are turned into cheap assassins, I focus on the visual aspects of the film, which underline the slow chipping away of innocence in children. This chapter, after exploring several aspects of psychological/emotional manipulation and how it finds itself fertile ground in hegemonic masculinity, goes on to investigate Jung's two main archetypes and one derivative: shadow; Trickster; and the devious cat. I finish the analysis with a nod to Neumann, saying that the supremacy of parents must end one way or the other for children to become independent individuals.

In Chapter 3, the boundaries between fiction and fact get even more blurry. Analysing both Paul Thomas Anderson's monumental human drama *Magnolia* (1999) and Michael Caton-Jones's adaptation of Tobias Wolff's own memoir *This Boy's Life* (1993), this chapter looks at the horrifying topic of child abuse perpetrated by parents. Covering emotional, physical, sexual, and financial abuse of children in detail, I investigate both the asymmetrical power relations between parents and children, and how being subjected to abuse as a child creates lost and broken adults. This chapter's discussion on abuse is also extended towards a doctor–patient context, referring to Jung's thorny affair with Sabina Spielrein, and it is wrapped with Jung's own perspective on parent–child relationships: that children are not the property of their parents.

In Chapter 4, parental abuse reaches its maximum and the most tragic outcome: domestic homicide. Using four different films on this gruesome topic – *The Shining* (1980), *Doctor Sleep* (2019), *Män som hatar kvinnor* (2009) (English title: *The Girl with the Dragon Tattoo*), and *Flickan som lekte med elden* (2009) (English title: *The Girl Who Played with Fire*) – this chapter investigates the motives behind both filicide and patricide. Focusing on complex legal and psychosocial aspects of murder in families, I weave in several plot lines from these four films to explore both Jungian and post-Jungian perspectives on patricide, how paternal hatred, how a devouring, cruel father would ultimately cause an equally destructive reaction and bring about his own death in the hands of his child.

Chapter 5, as the final story chapter, focuses on fathers who act as mentors for their children. Walking a fine line between sympathy as well as unflinching violence, this archetypal father occupies the grey area between right and wrong, integrity and criminality, virtue and vice. Expanding on the complex narratives of two films, *The Accountant* (2016) and *Bloodline* (2018), I look at the needs of two special children: one autistic; and the other a victim of domestic violence who becomes a social worker, showing his murderous side only to other abusers. This chapter dwells on the shadows of Jung's wise old man and how this greyness can be inherited and repeated through generations.

Family can be a source of happiness and a source of horror at the same time. This book is a collection of horror stories diving straight into that source. Whether read by you or your father, whether picked up at bedtime or during the day, the educational value of these stories does not diminish. They are frightening, disturbing, offensive, repulsive. They are tragic, heartbreaking, and they rarely have a happy ending. Even when they do, they have that lingering sense of sorrow. Seen from the eyes of the children, the stories shine a light on the shadows of fathers who were, who are, expected to keep their children safe from harm or injury, yet become the primary source of injury and harm. If Brecht is right, if art is not a mirror which reflects reality but in fact a hammer which can be used to shape reality, then these stories are both. They reflect the reality of those children suffering at the hands of their fathers. They show you the wounds of those children. What you do with those hammers is up to you.

References

Filmography

The Accountant. (2016) Directed by G. O'Connor. USA.
Ad Astra. (2019) Directed by J. Gray. USA.
Bloodline. (2018) Directed by H. Jacobson. USA.
Doctor Sleep. (2019) Directed by M. Flanagan. USA.
Flickan som lekte med elden. (2009) Directed by D. Alfredson. Denmark, Sweden.
Magnolia. (1999) Directed by P. T. Anderson. USA.
Män som hatar kvinnor. (2009) Directed by N. A. Oplev. Denmark, Sweden.
Partisan. (2015) Directed by A. Kleiman. Australia.
The Shining. (1980) Directed by S. Kubrick. UK, USA.
This Boy's Life. (1993) Directed by M. Caton-Jones. USA.

Bibliography

Abramovitch, H. (1997) 'Images of "father" in psychology and religion', in M. E. Lamb (ed.) *The Role of Father in Child Development.* New York: John Wiley & Sons.

Berdahl, J. L., Cooper, M., Glick, P., Livingston R. W., and Williams, J. C. (2018) 'Work as a masculinity contest', *Journal of Social Issues*, 74(3), 422–448.

Boss, P. (2011) *Loving Someone Who Has Dementia: How to Find Hope while Coping with Stress and Grief.* San Francisco: Jossey-Bass.

Bowlby, J. (1958) 'The nature of the child's tie to his mother', *International Journal of Psychoanalysis*, 39, 350–371.

Breu, C. (2022) 'Rethinking masculinities studies', *American Literary History*, 34(2), 586–595.

Brott, A. A. and Rudick, J. A. (2021) *The Expectant Father: The Ultimate Guide for Dads-to-Be.* New York: Abbeville Press.

Bruzzi, S. (2005) *Bringing up Daddy: Fatherhood and Masculinity in Post-war Hollywood.* London: BFI Publishing.

Carrigan, T., Connell, R. W., and Lee, J. (1985) 'Towards a new sociology of masculinity', *Theory and Society*, 14(5), 551–604.

Charles, M. and Grusky, D. (2004) *Occupational Ghettos: The Worldwide Segregation of Women and Men.* Stanford: Stanford University Press.

Clatterbaugh, K. (1990) *Contemporary Perspectives on Masculinity.* Boulder: Westview Press.

Colman, A. and Colman, L. (1998) *The Father: Mythology and Changing Roles.* Wilmette: Chiron Publications.

Connell, R. W. (1995) *Masculinities.* Cambridge: Polity.

Coontz, S. (1992) *The Way We Never Were: American Families and the Nostalgia Trap.* New York: Basic Books.

Coontz, S. (2005) *Marriage: A History.* London: Penguin Books.

Corneau, G. (1991) *Absent Fathers, Lost Sons: The Search for Masculine Identity.* New York: Shambhala Publications.

Cowan, R. S. (1983) *More Work for Mother.* New York: Basic Books.

Crenshaw, K. (2017) *On Intersectionality: Essential Writings.* New York: The New Press.

Craig, S. (1992) *(ed.) Men, Masculinity and the Media.* London: Sage.

de Beauvoir, S. (1953) *The Second Sex.* New York: Alfred A. Knopf.

Dermott, E. (2008) *Intimate Fatherhood.* London: Routledge.

Doucet, A. (2006) *Do Men Mother?* Toronto: University of Toronto Press.

Emig, R. and Rowland, A. (2010) *Performing Masculinity.* New York: Palgrave Macmillan.

Featherstone, B. and White, S. (2006) 'Dads talk about their lives and services', in C. Ashley, B. Featherstone, C. Roskill, M. Ryan, and S. White, *Fathers Matter: Research Findings on Fathers and their Involvement with Social Care Services.* London: Family Rights Group, pp. 69–81.

Featherstone, B., Rivett, M., and Scourfield, J. (2007) *Working with Men in Health and Social Care.* London: Sage.

Felitti, V. J., Anda, R. F., Nordenberg, D., Williamson, D. F., Spitz, A. M., Edwards, V., Koss, M. P., and Marks, J. S. (1998) 'Relationship of childhood abuse and household dysfunction to many of the leading causes of death in adults: The adverse childhood experiences (ACE) study', *American Journal of Preventative Medicine,* 14 (4), 245–258.

Foster, C. (2020) *Narcissistic Fathers: How to Deal with a Toxic Father and Complex PTSD.* Independently published.

Freud, S. (1939) *Moses and Monotheism.* New York: Alfred A. Knopf.

Friedan, B. (1963) *The Feminine Mystique.* New York: W. W. Norton.

Frosh, S. (1997) 'Fathers' ambivalence (too)', in W. Hollway and B. Featherstone (eds) *Mothering and Ambivalence.* London: Routledge, pp. 37–54.

Gatrell, C. (2007) 'Whose child is it anyway? The negotiation of paternal entitlements within marriage', *The Sociological Review,* 55(2), 352–372.

Gilmore, D. D. (1990) *Manhood in the Making: Cultural Concepts of Masculinity.* New Haven: Yale University Press.

Giddens, A. (1992) *The Transformation of Intimacy: Sexuality, Love and Eroticism in Modern Societies.* Cambridge: Polity.

Greenstein, H. R. (1983) *Judaism: An Eternal Covenant.* Philadelphia: Fortress Press.

Greer, G. (1970) *The Female Eunuch.* London: MacGibbon & Kee.

Gurian, M. (1992) *The Prince and the King: Healing the Father–Son Wound, a Guided Journey of Initiation.* New York: G. P. Putnam's Sons.

Harlow, H. F. (1958) 'The nature of love', *American Psychologist,* 13(12), 673–685.

Hearn, J. (2002) 'Men, fathers and the state: national and global relations', in B. Hobson (ed) *Making Men into Fathers: Men, Masculinities and the Social Politics of Fatherhood.* Cambridge: Cambridge University Press, pp. 245–273.

Henwood, K. and Procter, J. (2003) 'The "good father": reading men's accounts of paternal involvement during the transition to first-time fatherhood', *British Journal of Social Psychology,* 42(3), pp. 337–355.

Hollis, J. (1994) *Under Saturn's Shadow: The Wounding and Healing of Men.* Toronto: Inner City Books.

Holter, Ø. G. (2005) 'Can men do it? On men, caring and gender equality in an East/West European perspective', in A. Tereškinas and J. Reingardienė (eds) *Men and Fatherhood: New Forms of Masculinity in Europe.* Vilnius: Eugrimas, pp. 114–145.

Hsu, K. and Iwamoto, D. K. (2014) 'Testing for measurement invariance in the Conformity to Masculine Norms – 46 across White and Asian American college men: Development and validity of the CMNI-29', *Psychology of Men & Masculinity*, 15, 397–406.

Jacoby, M. (1999) *Jungian Psychotherapy and Contemporary Infant Research Basic Patterns of Emotional Exchange.* London: Routledge.

Jung, C. G. (1967) *The Collected Works of C. G. Jung, Volume 5: Symbols of Transformation.* Princeton: Princeton University Press.

Jung, C. G. (1969) *The Collected Works of C. G. Jung, Volume 9 (Part 1): Archetypes and the Collective Unconscious.* Princeton: Princeton University Press.

Jung, C. G. (1970) *The Collected Works of C. G. Jung, Volume 11: Psychology and Religion: West and East.* Princeton: Princeton University Press.

Kilkey, M. and Clarke, H. (2010) 'Disabled men and fathering: opportunities and constraints', *Community, Work & Family*, 13(2), 127–146.

Kilkey, M., Plomien, A., and Perrons, D. (2014) 'Migrant men's fathering narratives, practices and projects in national and transnational spaces: recent Polish male migrants to London', *International Migration*, 52 (1), 178–191.

Kimmel, M. (2012) *Manhood in America.* New York: Free Press.

Kipinis, A. R. (1991) *Knights without Armor: A Practical Guide for Men in Quest of Masculine Soul.* New York: Tarcher/Perigee.

Lamb, M. E. (1997) *The Role of the Father in Child Development.* Chichester: Wiley.

Levant, R. F. (2011) 'Research in the psychology of men and masculinity using the gender role strain paradigm as a framework', *American Psychologist*, 66(8), 765–776.

Levant, R. F. and Richmond, K. (2007) 'A review of research on masculinity ideologies using the Male Role Norms Inventory', *The Journal of Men's Studies*, 15(2), 130–146.

Mahalik, J. R., Locke, B. D., Ludlow, L. H., Diemer, M. A., Scott, R. P., Gottfried, M., and Freitas, G. (2003) 'Development of the conformity to masculine norms inventory', *Psychology of Men & Masculinity*, 4, 3–25.

Miller, J. D., Hoffman, B. J., Gaughan, E. T., Gentile, B., Maples, J., and Campbell, W. K. (2011) 'Grandiose and vulnerable narcissism: A nomological network analysis', *Journal of Personality*, 79, 1013–1042.

Morgan, D. (1996) *Family Connections.* Cambridge: Polity.

Mullender, A., Hague, G., Imam, U., Kelly, L., Malos, E. and Regan, L. (2002) *Children's Perspectives on Domestic Violence.* London: Sage Publications.

Newman, S. (2003) *Nobody's Baby Now: Reinventing Your Adult Relationship with Your Mother and Father.* New York: Walker & Company.

O'Brien, M. (2005) *Shared Caring: Bringing Fathers into the Frame.* Norwich: University of East Anglia.

O'Brien, M. and Shemilt, I. (2003) *Working Fathers: Earning and Caring.* Manchester: Equal Opportunities Commission.

O'Neil, J. M. (2012) 'The psychology of men: Theory, research, clinical knowledge, and future directions', in E. Altmaier and J. Hansen (eds) *Oxford Handbook of Counseling Psychology.* New York: Oxford University Press, pp. 375–408.

O'Neil, J. M. (2015) *Men's Gender Role Conflict: Psychological Costs, Consequences, and an Agenda for Change*. Washington: American Psychological Association.

Parent, M. C. and Moradi, B. (2009) 'Confirmatory factor analysis of the conformity to masculine norms inventory and development of the conformity to masculine norms inven- tory-46', *Psychology of Men & Masculinity*, 10, 175–189.

Parsons, T. (1949) 'The social structure of the family', in R. N. Anshen (ed.) *The Family: Its Functions and Destiny*. New York: Harper & Bros.

Phillips, R. and Cree, V. (2014) 'What does the "Fourth Wave" mean for teaching feminism in 21st century social work?' *Social Work Education*, 33(7), 930–943.

Pleck, J. H. (1995) 'The gender role strain paradigm: An update', in R. F. Levant and W. S. Pollack (eds) *A New Psychology of Men*. New York: Basic Books, pp. 11–32.

Pleck, E. H. and Pleck, J. H. (1997) 'Fatherhood Ideals in the United States: Histor- ical Dimensions', in M. Lamb (ed.) *The Role of the Father in Child Development*. 3rd ed. New York: Wiley.

Popenoe, D. (1998) 'Life without father' in C. R. Daniels (ed.) *Lost Fathers: The Politics of Fatherlessness in America*. London: Macmillan, pp. 33–51.

Rice, S. M., Fallon, B. J., and Bambling, M. (2011) 'Men and depression: The impact of masculine norms throughout the lifespan', *The Australian Educational and Developmental Psychologist*, 28, 133–144.

Saitoti, T. O. (1986) *The worlds of a Maasai Warrior: An autobiography*. Berkeley: University of California Press.

Schwartz, S. E. (2020) *The Absent Father Effect on Daughters: Father Desire, Father Wounds*. New York: Routledge.

Scott, G. R. (1966) *Phallic Worship: A History of Sex and Sexual Rites*. London: Senate.

Sussman, H. L. (2012) *Masculine Identities: The History and Meanings of Manliness*. Santa Barbara: Praeger.

Tacey, D. (1997) *Remaking Men: Jung, Spirituality and Social Change*. New York: Routledge.

Thomas, E. M. (1959) *The Harmless People*. New York: Vintage Books.

Trepp, L. (1973) *A History of the Jewish Experience: Eternal Faith, Eternal People*. New York: Behrman.

van der Gaag, N. (2014) *Feminism and Men*. London: Zed Books.

Vandello, J. A., Bosson, J. K., Cohen, D., Burnaford, R. M. and Weaver, J. R. (2008) 'Precarious manhood', *Journal of Personality and Social Psychology*, 95(6), 1325–1339.

Wade, L. and Ferree, M. M. (2018) *Gender: Ideas, Interactions, Institutions*. 2nd ed. New York: Norton.

Weiner, M. O. and Gallo-Silver, L. P. (2019) *The Complete Father: Essential Concepts and Archetypes*. Jefferson: McFarland & Company.

Williams, C. (1995) *Still a Man's World*. Berkeley, CA: University of California Press.

Wilmer, H. A. (1987) *Practical Jung: Nuts and Bolts of Jungian Psychotherapy*. Wilmette: Chiron Publications.

Winnicott, D. W. (1967) *Playing and Reality*. London: Tavistock.

Wong, Y. J., Ho, M. R., Wang, S., and Miller, I. K. (2017) 'Meta-analyses of the relationship between conformity to masculine norms and mental health-related outcomes', *Journal of Counseling Psychology*, 64, 80–93.

Chapter 1

The absentee

In 1949, Joseph Campbell published his famous book *The Hero with a Thousand Faces* (Campbell, 1949), bringing different examples of hero myths from all around the world together. In this book, he discussed what he called the 'hero's journey' (or simply the *monomyth*) as a common archetypal narrative pattern which can be identified in several myths and stories, and he presented seventeen detailed stages of this journey categorised under three separate parts. According to this pattern, the first part is called 'Departure', where the protagonist of the story receives a call or some new information which prompts them to embark on an adventure and leave their daily routine. In the second part, called 'Initiation', they go through several trials and tribulations during this adventure and face this journey's main ordeal. Now victorious and with a reward out of that ordeal, the protagonist returns to his previous life in the third part, called 'Return', as a transformed, wiser person.

This narrative pattern concept of Campbell became very popular, but it was also met with counter-arguments. Criticised by Brin (1999) as promoting elitism, by Segal (1984) as being mainly Campbell's personal assertions and interpretations rather than a well-researched argument, and by Dundes (1984) as failing to acknowledge earlier studies of narrative patterns and hero traditions, the *monomyth* concept continued to be discussed and referenced. Following Campbell, Leeming (1981), Cousineau (1990), and Vogler (2007) presented their interpretations of this pattern, and they reduced the number of stages and renamed some of them. However, Campbell's original three-part structure (which are also called 'acts') remained as a helpful organisational perspective in discussing the hero's journey.

This structure appears to create the backbone of James Gray's 2019 science fiction film *Ad Astra* (2019). Premiered at the Venice Film Festival in August and internationally released a few months later, *Ad Astra* looks at a broken and dysfunctional father–son relationship against the backdrop of endless space. The film's title means 'to the stars' in Latin, and the storyline takes the protagonist from Earth to the outer reaches of the Solar System and brings him back as a psychologically transformed man after an emotionally difficult but honest encounter with his estranged father.

DOI: 10.4324/9781003394488-1

Produced, co-written, and directed by Gray, *Ad Astra* tells both the external and the internal journey of an astronaut named Roy McBride (Brad Pitt). Set in the late twenty-first century, the film depicts manned outposts on the Moon and Mars run both by civilian and army personnel working for a fictional organisation called SpaceCom. As a major in the US Air Force, Roy's professional life demands a strictly logical and an exceptionally calm demeanour. This manner, however, has also defined his interactions with everyone around him, making him emotionally dead externally and internally. As a consequence, his marriage ended, and his wife Eve (Liv Tyler) left him. Roy's life becomes upended when he is given a mission to investigate mysterious and electromagnetic power surges which threaten all life on Earth. Shortened as 'The Surge', this threat seems to originate from a spaceship called Lima, which is a part of a 29-year-old deep space mission called the Lima Project. Lima's antimatter chamber is assumed to be the reason behind the surges, and an uncontrolled release of the antimatter can cause a chain reaction which will destabilise the Solar System. Roy is assigned to go to Mars to try to communicate with his father, the commander of this project, H. Clifford McBride (Tommy Lee Jones), who was presumed dead and considered a hero all these years.

Roy travels to the Moon base first to get on the rocket to Mars with Colonel Pruitt (Donald Sutherland) who acts like a surrogate father to him. After the attack on the Moon, Pruitt is unable to accompany Roy to Mars, but reveals the secret mission objective that if he fails to communicate with his father SpaceCom will destroy Lima. Surviving another deadly attack on a biomedical spaceship, Roy finally arrives on the red planet, greeted by the facility director Helen Santos (Ruth Negga) who discloses more hidden information about Lima. She tells Roy that, sometime during the mission which her parents were a part of, the crew wanted to return home, but Roy's father went crazy and killed them all, making Helen an orphan. Because of this horrible event, SpaceCom now wants to bury all the evidence along with Clifford, as it will tarnish their reputation.

After the seemingly unsuccessful attempts to contact his father, Roy, with the help of Helen, boards the rocket to Neptune, which is loaded with nuclear munitions. During his solitary 79-day journey to the planet, Roy goes through long periods of reminiscing and examines his relationships with everybody. An old, worn-out, and mentally unstable Clifford greets him on Lima, and confesses that he did not really care about him or his mother, because his space missions were more important than them. As Roy realises it is not possible to convince him to come back to Earth, he lets him go, destroys Lima, and successfully completes his mission. He returns home as a changed man, now ready and willing to embrace an emotional depth he lacked in his human relationships. The film ends with him smiling as he makes amends with his ex-wife.

In the short documentary called *To the Stars* which is included on the Blu-Ray edition of the film, director James Gray explains that the name of the film is the shortened version of the phrase 'Ad astra per aspera', meaning 'A rough road leads to the stars'. This phrase also appears on the Apollo 1 memorial plaque at the Cape Canaveral Launch Complex 34 in Florida, serving as a reminder for the courage, hardships, and the tragic death of Command Pilot Gus Grissom, Senior Pilot Ed White, and Pilot Roger Chaffee.

A rough road to the stars is indeed the main story backbone of Gray's film. Gray, however, creates a doubly perilous journey for his fictional character, Roy. Every step of the way, Roy faces physically challenging situations to stay alive and complete the mission, and is also forced to undergo an onerous internal transformation under the weight of his past. This two-layered journey reaches its zenith with his unavoidable confrontation with his father which helps him reform his outlook on life and change certain patterns of behaviour he adopted as a son.

This cinematic depiction of inner growth/maturation appears to be an extension of the director's own experiences. In the same documentary, Gray candidly talks about how he lost his mother when he was very young and how he finds the notion of closure nonsensical. He argues that people have the ability to learn to live with terrible things that happen to them, but overall, they cannot find or achieve closure. He also admits that *Ad Astra* is his personal deep dive, marking his own position in time during his life journey, reflecting where he was and how he was during the making of the film.

Within this context, the film becomes an interesting and intimate case study of the deeply frayed bonds between absent parents and their children which continue to echo in the fabric of space and time in different ways. The unlived, unfulfilled relationship between Clifford and Roy as father and son becomes an artistic metaphor, an imaginative meditation on the nature of negative fathers. As Roy travels all the way to Neptune to stop his father from destroying the Solar System, his philosophical musings about himself, fatherhood, and relationships turn *Ad Astra* into a unique example of cinematic portrayal where a fictional character mirrors the real-life difficulties of people fighting the emotional toll of parental absence. In other words, Roy's Campbellian departure, initiation, and return convey more than its plain narrative content.

In order to mirror Gray's deep dive, this chapter will explore the film's multi-layered storyline in three parts. The first part will focus on the visual symbolism and will examine some of the mythological and astrological contents. The second part will investigate how the absence of parents affect children both mentally and emotionally. The last part will highlight the Jungian content in relation to Roy's development both as a child and as a man.

Symbols from the Earth all the way to the stars

In 2022, James Gray revealed to *The Hollywood Reporter* that as the film's director he was not given a chance to deliver *Ad Astra*'s final cut before its release, and he compares this painful experience to losing a loved one (Abramovitch, 2022). Even though he did not have control over the end product, he certainly created a visually impressive backdrop to an emotionally challenging story, mixing science and logic with heart and wonder.

Roy's internal and external journeys which take place simultaneously in the film follow completely opposite directions until the finale. The further he goes from the Earth physically, the closer he gets home emotionally and discovers what is meaningful to him. After this difficult and crucial process of personal change and development is complete, he comes back to Earth. By ending up where everything started, he finishes one symbolic cycle of his life, and starts another one with the acquired wisdom of the last. In this circular narrative, Gray uses a combination of ordinary and iconic visual symbols which appear throughout the film. These are: door/gate; ship/vehicle; the Moon; ape/monkey; Mars; and Neptune.

Ad Astra's depiction of futuristic space exploration features two specific and recurring images. The first is the door/gate imagery. From the first four minutes until almost the very last shot of the film, Roy is shown either opening doors, passing through gates, or being next to one. This repetitive visual language is used regardless of his location: on the International Space Antenna (04:44); during the spacewalk scene to reach Vesta IX (40:01); or when he boards Lima (86:02). He repeatedly opens spacecraft hatches, walks through doors or gates, or waits for someone to open them for him to be able to continue his journey.

Doors and gates are indeed symbols of travel, an act of crossing, roaming, passage and voyage, from one state to another, sometimes from a known world to an unknown one. They appear as lines, edges, thresholds which must be crossed in order to either continue a movement or to initiate one. As Biedermann (1996a) notes, they are associated with the notion of transition. He also quotes the famous journalist and author Algernon Blackwood regarding the symbolism of doors. According to Blackwood, behind every door there is a new space with different conditions, people, or situations (ibid., p. 151). Therefore, crossing these thresholds also leads to different states of consciousness and being.

Jung wrote about doors and mentioned their symbolic meaning within the context of religious and psychological processes of becoming conscious, individuation, and rebirth (CW 9ii, para. 312; CW 9i, para. 45). He argued that the shadow is a small, constricted pathway into a deep, boundless well of information and life where one's self encounters something it believed it was not, where 'I' discovers the other, where people become aware of the fact that they are made up of indivisible parts, both light and dark. In the film, Roy's physical journey to Neptune leads to his self-discovery and a psychological rejuvenation following his final meeting with Clifford which transpires in a rather spiritual fashion, all happening against an endless cosmic background where celestial bodies are present but silent and indifferent.

During this challenging journey Roy is shown to use several means of transport, both on land and in space. Apart from the car he drives on Earth, and the rovers on both the Moon and Mars, he is repeatedly depicted in different spaceships or capsules. Symbolic tradition recognises ships as vessels of transport with a specific aim, destination, and course. As Chevalier and Gheerbrant (1996a) note, ships evoke the notion of strength, safety, movement, and danger, all embedded in sea voyages as well as space flights. The fact that a ship's (or a boat's) structural integrity can be torn apart by the force of water makes journeys over water both exciting and perilous. Ships, as in Noah's Ark, carry life, hope, faith and courage for a new beginning. They also carry diseases, pirates, war, and death with them. People can get lost trying to cross deep seas or find calm and peace where their troubles slowly dissolve as they sail through water's domain. Jung's dream analyses point out the relationship between vehicles and ego, reflecting aspects of individuals' inner lives and their transformational journey in time (CW 12, para. 153).

To represent this journey in time, the Moon and its phases are also used commonly throughout the world. Regularly in flux and renewing its observational shape in every 28 days, the Moon, just like four seasons, symbolises passing time. But because it disappears from the sky every lunar month for a few days, it is linked to death and rebirth, periodically and constantly following each other. Linked with the menstrual cycle and the fact that it receives and reflects the light of the Sun instead of emitting light of its own, the Moon is considered feminine, Yin, receptive, and passive. This light-reflecting quality becomes a symbol of knowledge and wisdom which can be acquired by reflection and contemplation (Chevalier and Gheerbrant, 1996b). As it influences the movements of tides and ebb and flow, it is considered as the ruler of the water element, a symbol of fluctuating emotions. Biedermann (1996b) also mentions the modern astrological view of the Moon, that it can affect a woman's external behaviour and personality, but it deeply affects a man's soul.

Roy arrives at the Moon quite early in the film, with mixed feelings both about the mission and his father. In tune with both the second act of 'hero's journey' and the Moon symbolism, his trials and tribulations start here. Colonel Pruitt is mindful of Roy's internal conflict, and he does not hide the fact that he is there to watch over him, something Clifford never did. This perceptive tenderness of Pruitt becomes the main trigger of Roy's slowly evolving contemplation which examines both himself and Clifford as two different men until the end of the film. When Pruitt is forced to stay on the Moon due to his irregular heartbeat, a result of a narrow escape, he tells Roy that SpaceCom does not trust Roy's abilities to complete the mission, making him feel further estranged from the deeply masculine and emotion-free world of the armed forces. This revelation results in Roy becoming more disobedient, especially symbolised by his clandestine rejection of taking mood-stabilisers, a strict SpaceCom requirement in space missions. Without an artificial chemical in his body, Roy gradually becomes more open and receptive towards acknowledging and accepting his own emotions from this point onwards, and discovers that vulnerability is also a strength in itself.

The constant threat of death inherent in Roy's mission continues to manifest beyond the Moon as well. After skilfully subduing the pirates on the Moon (who attack, smuggle, or kill for profit, exploiting the border disputes), Roy gets on another spaceship called Cepheus with a crew of four (who dutifully take their prescribed mood-stabilisers in order to stay calm and focused). When an emergency transmission is intercepted on their way to Mars, Roy and Tanner (Donnie Keshawarz), the captain of Cepheus, board Vesta IX, a biomedical research vessel orbiting asteroid Toro. As they try to locate the crew, Roy notices the scratches on the walls, indicating trouble and a possible attack. Within a couple of minutes, Tanner is violently killed by a baboon, and Roy kills another one while trying to recover Tanner's body.

Apes and monkeys (in general, primates), just like the Moon, bring opposite symbolic meanings together. For example, in ancient Egypt, Thoth, the god of wisdom, knowledge, and science, was depicted as a baboon with a lunar disc on his head. In ancient India, the ape-god Hanumān, Rama's divine assistant, herald and the patron god of martial arts, appears as the symbol of loyalty, self-control, and strength. While the Aztecs and Mayans associated monkeys with industrious and skilful craftsmen, in ancient Greece they were linked with pranks and mischief (hence, the Trickster archetype), especially within the myth of the Cercopes. With the arrival of Judeo-Christan and Islamic iconography, monkeys became the symbol of humanity corrupted by sin as well as the lust, greed, and the destructive capabilities of man (Biedermann, 1996c; Chevalier and Gheerbrant, 1996c; Ronnberg and Martin, 2010). The psychological link between monkey and the unregulated realm of the unconscious also suggests the unexpected (but beneficial) release of desires, sudden inspiration and insight. Ronnberg and Martin (ibid.) also point out the connection of monkeys with the theory of evolution, and how monkeys can also represent an out-of-control patriarchy.

Gray's chilling depiction of ferocious space baboons becomes multi-dimensional in this context. It is important to note that the attack scene takes place on a spaceship called Vesta, named after the goddess of home and family in Roman religion. Even though not shown directly, it is hinted that this spaceship might be conducting biomedical research on animals which might be deemed unethical on Earth. Therefore, for the pursuit of knowledge and science, these primates were probably used as lab animals, and now they attack every human they see with rage. In Roy's perspective, the rage he saw in those baboons becomes another eye-opening perspective during his post-attack psychological evaluation scene on Cepheus (45:48). In this scene Roy, without any mood-stabiliser in his system, suddenly shares a lot of information about his emotions, the way he, as a child, saw that rage in his father, how he felt about his abandonment, and how keeping these feelings repressed makes him, now as an adult male, unable to form loving and meaningful relationships with other people. In other words, Roy feels that his idea of a stable, loving home was violated by his father's absence. Therefore, his encounter with a violent primate provides him a clear, deep, and an unexpected understanding of his complicated problem: learning how not to be like his father while finding the balance between mind and heart, fortitude and defencelessness, masculine and feminine.

Roy's internal odyssey of discovering a new form of manliness reaches a new point as he lands on Mars. On Ersa station, the last manned post in the Solar System, Helen Santos shows him the final transmission of Clifford from 20+ years ago which is now a top-secret military file. In this message, Clifford, with an eerily calm manner, explains how the crew of Lima could not endure the psychological stress of being away from home and they attempted to turn back. As mission commander, he says, he did not give permission and killed them all, because the mission objective of finding alien intelligence was more important. By revealing this information, Helen makes it clear that Roy is not the only child orphaned by his father's actions. She does not blame or attack Roy for what Clifford did. She just proves that Clifford is only made a hero by SpaceCom because they wanted to protect themselves from public humiliation and lawsuits.

Quoting the astrology publications of Johann Wilhelm Andreas Pfaff, one of Germany's most eminent astronomers and mathematicians during the nineteenth century, Biedermann (1996d) describes Mars as the planet of tyrants, strife, and unpredicted catastrophes. Mars has indeed been the symbol of masculine energy, armed forces, and aggressive sexuality since ancient times. It is directly associated with murderous rage, passion, and competitive attitudes due to its red glow. However, these qualities come mainly from ancient Greek myths of Ares, the Olympian god of war and courage. While Ares inflicted punishment and was the avenger of crimes (Chevalier and Gheerbrant, 1996d), Romans preferred to highlight his harvest protection abilities, and therefore Mars was also worshipped as the god of agriculture and springtime. He was considered as the divine protector of youth and the guide of young men who leave their homes to build a new settlement of their own (ibid.).

Ad Astra certainly uses the complex symbolism of this mythical masculinity to highlight Roy's evolving inner self. By observing how Helen gives voice to her wounded self in a non-threatening way in order to connect with another person after such a traumatic parental loss, he becomes gradually more in tune with his ability to acknowledge and verbalise his feelings. His complete immersion in water during the underground lake scene just before he leaves Mars (69:00) becomes almost like a second baptism, symbolising his rebirth in a new world, a more balanced world of masculine behaviour and norms, a world his father was never a part of, and a world he is slowly building for himself.

On Mars, Roy sends two messages to his father, now orbiting Neptune. The first one is written by SpaceCom, a short, businesslike script with no personal touches. On his second attempt, Roy goes off script (against his orders) and sends an intimate and loving message to Clifford. This angers the company and he is removed from the mission immediately. Helen, seeing him as another victim of the Lima Project, takes Roy to the rocket, now leaving for Neptune with nuclear munitions on board. Roy promises Helen to deal with his father without elaborating on his only two options: either bring him to justice for his crimes or kill him.

This is probably why the planet Neptune, with its mesmerising blue hue, the place where Roy's main ordeal awaits him, appears towards the end of the film. Being composed of mainly gases and liquids, Neptune is the fourth largest and the farthest known planet of the Solar System. Named after the Roman god of the sea, Neptune takes the symbology of deep and mysterious waters to their absolute end. Greene (1996) mentions man's powerful yearning for redemption that can only be found in prenatal waters – either maternal or cosmic. In this sense, Neptune becomes the recurrent universal symbol of unifications and dissolutions. Furthermore, Chevalier and Gheerbrant (1996e) mention the connections between psychological states and Neptune's astrological symbolism – the mysterious blue planet governs the subconscious, can influence mental health negatively by mystification, triggering thoughts and emotions that may not be based on reality, and as a result, it is the harbinger of depression, irrational behaviour, neurosis, and schizophrenia. Due to the fact that it appears on the edge of the Solar System, it is the symbol of a dissolving logic and reason now flowing into an endless cosmic sea where one's self becomes aware of what is beyond, where ego and non-ego fuses, where one is lost but become one with the universe. It manifests in selfless, charitable acts, and participation in a bigger community. Biedermann (1996e) also refers to Neptune's famous trident, his three-pronged fishing spear, and its connection with the Hindu god Shiva, symbolising three different states and periods of time: creation/past; being/present; and destruction/future.

The final meeting and the parting of Roy and Clifford take place in Neptune's orbit, bringing a bittersweet redemption to both men. An old, weary, and non-compos mentis Clifford reveals that Lima could not find any sign of intelligent life in the universe, making his sacrificial killing of his crew in the name of science meaningless. When Roy gently tries to get him back to Cepheus to return home, he decides to untether himself and floats away into deep space, leaving a devastated son behind. However, his refusal to go back to Earth and his complete rejection of a close human connection helps Roy understand the value of meaningful human bonds in a universe where no other intelligent life exists. When Roy finally reaches the Earth, his final psychological evaluation proves how much he is willing now not to be like his father. He says he will rely on loved ones, and he will actively participate in making those relationships deep and sincere. In other words, the ripple effects of Clifford's physical and emotional absence are now transformed into Roy's physical and emotional presence in his community as a wiser man.

Ad Astra pays attention to the complex problem of a father's absence, his unwillingness to form a meaningful bond with his child, and the great lengths his son would go to in order to find a sense of resolution. The fact that the story plays out against a cosmic background makes the visual narrative even more majestic. However, Gray never deviates from his main focus: how can a son come to terms with a father who is not interested in his wellbeing? Are sons destined to mimic their fathers, their achievements, and mistakes? Or with every new experience, do people get a new chance to adapt and evolve? The next section will explore these questions within the context of the absent father syndrome.

Is closure nonsense? Anticlimactic resolutions with the absent father

As mentioned earlier, Gray thinks that closure is a great notion, but in reality, it does not exist. Based on his personal experience of growing up without a mother, he argues that a sense of a meaningful conclusion, a feeling that an emotional or traumatic experience has been settled or resolved in a satisfying way simply stems from impractical wishes. While this perspective is open to debate, his storyline and Roy's journey builds on it, and goes to highlight the ripple effects of growing up without a father, how that void in children grows when there is a lack of fatherly love.

The *Oxford English Dictionary* defines the word 'neglect' based on two different situations, one in action and the other non-active. The first situation refers to the state of not giving enough care or attention to something or somebody. In the second situation, neglect refers to the state of not receiving enough care or attention. Therefore, the notion of neglect covers both a failure in active behaviour and a deficiency in receiving. Generally defined as an unmet need (Daniel, 2015) and included under the umbrella term 'adverse childhood experiences'[1] (ACE) (Felitti et al., 1998; Reuben et al., 2016), experiencing neglect during childhood may increase adults' risk for disease and dysfunction later in life (Howe, 2005; Horwath, 2007; Radford et al., 2011; Corby et al., 2012). Bellis et al. (2014) also point out the increasing probability of people who experienced four or more of these adverse events during childhood becoming heavy drinkers and/or suicidal as adults.

Neglect can be physical, emotional, medical, educational, and social. Being a form of parental deprivation, it disrupts the healthy physical and emotional development of children. Even though Blechman (1982) argued that research into the psychological risks of children reared by one parent were inconclusive, researchers have demonstrated that father absence negatively influenced the cognitive development of girls and boys[2] (Santrock, 1972), resulting in lower IQ and achievement scores. From a neuropsychology perspective, early childhood neglect is also associated with changes in the prefrontal cortex which may influence persistent cognitive deficits (Hanson et al., 2013).

Ad Astra opens with a statement saying that the story takes place in the near future when humanity is observing the stars to find intelligent life and a sign of further progress. Ironically, it later becomes clear that this task of finding new intelligent life forms and thus taking humanity further is given to a man who was never interested in his own wife and son, and had no trouble finding his crew expendable. In other words, Clifford's neglect towards his family, something he openly admits without any remorse, morphed into a lethal disdain for his colleagues when they disagreed with him. Even though there is no information about Clifford's childhood in the film, he is described by several characters as a space legend, a hero, the most decorated officer, and an inspiration for the next generation of astronauts. While these descriptions paint a picture of a man who seems exceptionally capable of displaying knowledge, efficiency, and leadership, the way he behaves in the film implies he is suffering from narcissistic personality disorder.

Narcissism is an unhealthy form of self-absorption, a pathological personality trait. First identified by Havelock Ellis in 1898 (Morrison, 1986) in the form of excessive masturbation, narcissism is considered a disorder in DSM-5 which is characterised by feelings of pompousness, entitlement, limited or no empathy, fantasies of unlimited power, beauty, immortality etc., need for admiration and praise, and hostile/aggressive behaviour, especially when challenged (American Psychiatric Association, 2013). Generally classified in two variants, vulnerable (fragile/covert) or grandiose/malignant (Miller et al., 2011), the core drive of narcissistic behaviour is a profound sense of insecurity (Campbell and Foster, 2007). In order to cover up this lack of inner security and self-worth, narcissists act like the most confident person in the world blessed with the greatest of successes ever known to man. In their own universe, they are not even the next best thing after God, they are gods themselves. Therefore, anybody and anything is less important, less valuable, less deserving, and less relevant. In other words, simply less.

There are three specific scenes in the film which shine a light on Clifford's psyche: his final video message to Roy before he disappeared 29 years ago (15:08); his last and classified video message to SpaceCom after he killed his crew (64:30); and the scene where he explains how he saw Roy, his mother, and Earth on Lima (90:49). In his final message to Roy, Clifford tells how his spaceship is gone past Jupiter and heading towards Neptune. With enthusiasm in his voice, he explains how their journey to the edge of the heliosphere will finally answer the age-old question of whether there is another intelligent life form in the universe. He says he feels God's presence, now so far away from Earth. The message ends abruptly with him saying 'I love you' to Roy. In the second video file, which Roy did not know about until he was shown by Helen, Clifford appears with a serious but a completely calm face, announcing that he has killed his crew, innocent and guilty together, because they simply could not understand the importance of the mission and wanted to return. He adds he is forever driven on this quest and will carry on no matter what. In the last scene where the father and son cautiously meet on Lima, Clifford simply and coldly confirms what Roy knew deep down for years: that there was nothing for him on Earth, including his wife and son; that he never cared about them or their small ideas on Earth; and he did not think about home once while he was gone for 30 years.

The recurrent theme in these messages and his behaviour is condescendence. Even though he says he loves Roy very briefly in the first one, it rather looks like he is saying that because he is expected to say it as a father, rather than really meaning it. There is almost no affection in his voice, no other meaningful context is added, there is nothing that suggests a deep, sincere bond between him and Roy. As a contrast, he sounds genuinely excited about the mission which makes it clear that he is truly more interested in the mission itself, his own pursuit of success than his own son. It is also striking that there is no mention of his wife in this message. She is clearly not an object of interest, not to mention affection, even though she is left with the task of looking after Roy.

In the second message, his contempt for his crew is revealed through his choice of words: he says they were unable to cope with the psychological difficulty of being away from Earth. By describing his crew as feeble, sensitive, and inefficient, and by declaring his resolve to complete the mission on his own, he not only justifies his killings, but he also presents himself as the strongest person who meets the tough requirements of the mission. The fact that he killed everyone on the ship, insubordinate or not, makes it clear that other people on Lima were like objects to him, useful tools which were discarded without hesitation when they malfunctioned, broke down, or simply refused to bend to his will.

Of course, for Roy, his final meeting with Clifford proves to be the most difficult task emotionally. The way Clifford admits what he truly thought of him, his mother, and other people on Earth, how he knowingly and willingly abandoned them, how they never meant anything to him, and how his destiny is in the stars and not with them is truly heartless, something no son, no child would want to hear. However, it is the core of Roy's problem: facing the horror, the reality of being unwanted, unloved, unneeded. Now understanding why he could not form a meaningful bond with his father, and seeing it was not his own fault, Roy realises that he could fight against anything, anything that is present, but he could not fight against what is absent.

Eva Seligman (1985, 2018) calls these types of children 'the half-alive ones'. Specifically referring to fathers who were experienced as unavailable by the mother and the child, she argues that children of these types of men grow up to be adults who are unable to enjoy social contacts. Deprived of the experience of having a nurturing father, they run the risk of being suffocated by an all-enveloping motherly love, a psychological fusion with the mother even though physically separate, hence making them unable to confirm and articulate their own identity and needs in relationships. Of course, while this perspective focuses on father's absence and its ripple effects, it does not look at the reason behind the absence. In the case of *Ad Astra*, the reasons behind Clifford's intentional unavailability and neglect suggest that symptoms of narcissistic personality disorder play a part.

The 'half-alive' description also fits in well with the results of the mandatory medication procedures for astronauts which are repeatedly observed in the film. These astronauts, including Roy, are required to take mood stabilisers during their missions in order to dull their possible emotional highs and lows. While this procedure prevents any unsettling fluctuations which might endanger themselves, their colleagues, and their missions, it also turns them into rather unfeeling, indifferent, and emotionally flat people. It is important to note that only after Roy repeatedly refuses to take his medication, he gets in touch with his feelings more freely and becomes more expressive which gradually brings about his much-needed enjoyment in close relationships. In the case of Clifford, these medications might have contributed to his disorder, making him even more uncaring and inhumane.

Is there a way to tip the balance against deep feelings of parental neglect? Is there any hope for children who had the misfortune of having a narcissistic father who not only abandons them but also describes them as insignificant when they face him years later? The answer is not a straightforward yes or no. As Balcom (1998) notes, not every son suffers from the absence of his father. However, Balcom also mentions the studies of Bartholomew (1990) and Byng-Hall (1991), and argues that paternal absence affects sons' self-worth, and because these children feel abandoned and suffer from a cryptic loss, their ability to initiate and sustain intimate relationships is hampered. Therefore, their cryptic mourning (Abraham and Torok, 1994; Holmwood, 2023) must be acknowledged, its buried components of shame, rage, or simply unrequited love must be unearthed and worked through in order for these children to heal.

In the film, Roy appears to be on the receiving end of childhood neglect due to his father's narcissism. Clifford's needs, even though he is the parent, takes precedence over the needs of Roy. The studies of Monk (2001) and Crocker (2009) have shown that children of narcissistic parents have a variety of problems in their adult years, including mood, anxiety, and post-traumatic stress disorders as well as self-doubt and intimacy issues. These children either grow up to be people pleasing adults who have internalised a drive to sabotage their happiness in order to make others happy or learn to be narcissistic in order to survive – in other words, mimic the parent. Roy appears to display a combination of these outcomes. For example, during his first psychological evaluation at the very beginning of the film where his wife leaves him for being emotionally empty and distant, he says he is extremely committed to his job as a major, determined not to be distracted by anything or anyone else. This shows that he is not only following the footsteps of his father, being a perfect officer in the military and pleasing his superiors, but also sacrificing his family life and happiness instead of forming meaningful bonds. His recovery, however, only starts after he stops taking his mood-stabilisers (which is basically a physical defiance of military authority and an end to his people-pleasing) and aims to re-unite with his father and bring him back home peacefully (which is an attempt to repair a broken bond).

Unfortunately, whatever hope he might have had regarding Clifford (and alleviating his own yearning for fatherly love) gets shattered first by Clifford's merciless declaration, and then his suicide. Being accepted and embraced as he is by his son is impossible for Clifford to tolerate. Therefore, he prefers oblivion instead of a meaningful bond. This is probably why Ethan Gross, who wrote the script with Gray, finds the conclusion rather anticlimactic. Because it becomes clear that there is no chance of a satisfying resolution both for the father and the son. In other words (and as Gray suggests), there is no closure for Roy, no fulfilment out of this reunion, no rekindling of a fatherly love he dearly needs – only an irrefutable, unchangeable fact that he must learn to live with, without letting Clifford's absence affect and dictate how he forms his future relationships, both with himself and others.

Roy certainly returns home from Neptune as a changed, wise(r) man. As mentioned earlier, this is particularly depicted in his last psychological evaluation which wraps up the film. Sticking to the hero's journey concept, Gray gives his protagonist a more mature and confident masculinity which is in touch with his feelings, rather than shunning or repressing them. He chooses not to mimic his father, decides to actively engage with people empathically, and therefore manages to evolve and adapt. The next section will explore this inner transformation from a Jungian perspective.

Sharing burdens: dissolving boundaries and learning to connect

Jung wrote both about his father who was a clergyman and the father archetype. He had a more stable relationship with his father compared to his mother who was depressed and hospitalised (Jung, 1989). While he observed mood swings and unpredictability in his mother, he experienced a better sense of order and stability through his father. When he wrote about the father archetype, he associated it with *yang* (CW 10, para. 65), the male and active cosmic principle in Chinese philosophy. He argued that this archetype determines everyone's connections and dealings with men, the law, the state, authority, power, rationality, and the mind, evoking the ancient cultural associations with the Sun god. Rules, regulations, and boundaries are all related to the father archetype. Jung even mentioned the notion 'Fatherland', not only suggesting a specific place in space and time, but also highlighting where the power of the state is most visible.

Ad Astra plays on these different associations in interesting ways. For example, clearly defined state borders of the Earth do not mean anything on the Moon, not only giving rise to pirate activity and lawlessness but also suggesting how these states' power wane beyond Earth. Plus, in the film there is the constant presence of SpaceCom, representing armed forces and military prowess, a symbol of authority, command, and rules. Clifford, Pruitt, and Roy disobey its rules and regulations in different ways throughout the film, indicating their personal psychological interaction with this archetype. But undeniably, at its core, the film explores how the absence of a father can be as negative and unhelpful as the presence of one.

Schwartz (2021) focuses on this absence from daughters' perspective and explores how the loss and longing for an absent father can damage the female psyche within a Jungian framework. Quoting Hillman (1989), she writes that the wounding caused by their father's non-existence creates feelings of futility, recurring periods of meaninglessness, and a psyche pulled in different directions where personal needs and inner rage may never be expressed or fulfilled for these daughters. Of course, these perspectives apply for sons too. As explored in the last section, children, regardless of their gender, are prone to psychological injuries when their fathers are absent.

The perspectives of sons are further explored by another Jungian analyst. In his chapter aptly titled *Father Hunger*, Hollis (1994) describes how sons are driven to father figures when the real father is unavailable. These figures can be false and deceptive like inspiring religious figures[3], popular stars, or even political ideologies. Sons are driven to these figures because, as Hollis argues (ibid., p. 89), every son needs to hear that they are loved and accepted as they are by their own father. Obviously, 'hearing' refers not just to a simple verbal affirmation, but to the whole experience of being acknowledged and supported as a child. If this experience is derailed, it triggers a father hunger which compels these children to either alter their own nature to win their father's approval (i.e. people pleasing), or they resort to self-blame thinking they are unworthy or they are the reason behind their father's absence. In short, their individuality is repressed which leads to complex mental health problems.

In the film, Roy is depicted as a child who followed the footsteps of his father and became successful in the military, sacrificing not just his marriage in the process but also his need to bond with another person. His short, unexpected, but important contact with Pruitt, who represents a caring father figure, contributes to his repressed feelings and needs resurfacing. The importance of this encounter becomes more apparent when Roy travels to Neptune all alone on Cepheus. He finds the chance to revisit his memories and experiences during this solitary journey which turns into a rather monastic experience of self-discovery and analysis without being disturbed or interrupted. His physical journey to find and meet his lost father is juxtaposed with his symbolic inner journey which turns out to be his discovery of himself.

Gray provides information about this inner journey in several scenes scattered throughout the film, either in Roy's speeches or inner-monologues: Roy says how he has screwed up by being harsh when he should have been caring

(18:32); how he believed Clifford's empty promises (36:48); how he specifically pursued a career which his father would approve of (56:48); how he was self-ish and let others down (79:57); and how he was terrified to confront his father all his life (83:24).

This difficult but honest self-analysis becomes the visible proof of a child who not only suffered from his father's absence deeply but is also in the process of overcoming the personal consequences and limitations of this suffering. This process reaches its culmination when he finally reaches Neptune. As a visual hint, Gray shows the two spacecrafts, Lima and Cepheus, in the same frame going in opposite directions – like father and son – against the cold, blue backdrop of the planet (82:41). As mentioned earlier, Neptune is the symbol of unifications and dissolutions. It is where logic and reason end, the feelings rule, the boundaries dissolve in an endless, mysterious ocean, turning life into a transcendent experience.

Up until the crucial moment in the film where Roy and Clifford finally meet, Gray plays with the expectation that the longing of the son would finally be over, that Roy's 'father hunger' would finally be satisfied by his apologetic, repentant father, and that the two would rekindle their bond in an eternal embrace witnessed by the universe. Fortunately, in Gray's world realism prevails, and Clifford lays bare his innermost feelings in an interesting plot twist, an unexpected – but necessary – wake-up call for Roy to turn his life around. As Clifford's boundless, and now unconstrained selfishness takes centre stage, there is nothing left for Roy but to acknowledge his error of trying to be like his father, and the error of expecting love from a person who is unable to give it.

So, how can these children heal themselves when they are wounded by their own absent fathers who refused – and continue to refuse – to be present? Hollis (ibid., p. 92) argues that boys grow up only when they leave home psychologically, meaning not just a childlike venture into the unknown but a deliberate act to be independent from the (sometimes pacifying) comfort and the protection of the mother–father dyad. Boys/men must learn the art of self-compassion, self-care, and self-nourishment. In other words, they must take the responsibility of their own care, provide themselves with what they have not been provided in order to transcend the crippling dependency. This does not mean an overcompensation on a personal path to become a self-sufficient recluse. It means mastering the balance between independence and receiving support.

After all, it is crucial for every child to acknowledge and claim their own individuality. Even though they are the product of a union between their mother and father, they are neither the extensions of them nor copies. They are new, unique individuals which they must learn to become and be comfortable in being. In the case of absent fathers, the authentic selves of these children are hidden behind their false selves, in other words persona, which Jung described as an outer shell, a psychological mechanism to adapt to the world (CW 6, para. 801), a mechanism perceived as genuine by all (CW 9i, para. 221). Only by discarding this persona can children recover their authentic selves and fully grow up.

It is also important to remember what Corneau (1991) said about absent fathers and lost sons. Sons need to connect with their own vulnerabilities, face their own fears if they want to heal from the wounding of their absent fathers. This approach, Corneau argued, helps them become more tolerant not only of themselves but also others. *Ad Astra* depicts this process quite openly. When Clifford tells Roy he simply did not care about him, Roy replies with an infinitely sad 'I know but I still love you' (91:13), facing his most difficult ordeal but responding with the compassion and tolerance he was never shown. Of course, his reply is not another act to please Clifford. Roy really means it. By doing this he not only proves that he is different from his father, but he also discards his persona and reclaims his authentic self. He truly becomes the kind, compassionate man he has always been deep inside but unable to admit or show it.[4] When he returns home after Clifford's suicide, during his last psychological evaluation (111:40), he articulates his intention to continue being that man, to share the burdens of the people close to him and let them share his, to live and love.

Jung defines this internal transformation process as individuation (CW 6, paras 757–762). Individuation includes a combination of things: personality development; mutual relationships; and a defiance of social norms that are fixed and intransigent. Through his solitary journey to the edge of the Solar System and back, by both physically and psychologically letting go of his absent father who refuses to be with him, and by recognising and appreciating the importance of meaningful human bonds (which runs contrary to the reason why he was selected for this military mission in the first place), Roy learns how to individuate. He willingly breaks down the barriers he built around himself. He is now open to connect to others. He finds his own balance between absence and presence, cold logic and feeling, yin and yang.

From being a half-alive child to a mature man who is not afraid to articulate and show his feelings, Roy completes his personal 'hero's journey' as a transformed, psychologically rejuvenated person. As Brad Pitt mentions in the short documentary called *A Man Named Roy*, also included on the Blu-Ray edition, Roy sees the weaknesses of a repressed and trapped masculine mindset and chooses to evolve. This is probably why the film ends with him smiling and reuniting with his ex-wife. Instead of being physically and emotionally unavailable like his father, he is now aware of his capacity to receive and give love. Instead of being full of rage and destructive like Ares, he starts to build the 'home' he needs, reconstruct his life in a better way like Mars.

From absent father to manipulating father

Regarding other intelligent life in the universe, Arthur C. Clarke once pointed out the only two possibilities, which are equally terrifying: that it existed or not. Through all the hardships to the stars depicted in the film, *Ad Astra* puts its bet on the latter. However, by emphasising the idea that in such an empty universe the loneliness is only bearable through forming and maintaining sincere and caring human connections, it upholds the sagacious idea of Carl Sagan (1986) that human beings, after all, are small creatures, and they can only endure the stupendous size of the universe through love.[5]

When released, the critics were quick to label the film's content as 'daddy issues in outer space' (Brooks, 2019; Gleiberman, 2019). A closer look underneath this correct label uncovers why Roy, as a son, was so damaged by his father and how he can help himself recover from this damage. He finds his answers after he travels nearly 3 billion miles from home and replaces the toxic absence of his father with the gentle and beneficial presence of other people who are willing to mirror his kindness and love. He learns that this is what makes his life, in fact any life, worth living.

It goes without saying that not only absent fathers have the potential to hurt and damage their children. Their presence can cause difficulties as well. The next chapter will flip the coin and explore aspects of narcissism in a different context. This time a boy will discover that how his seemingly loving and ever-present father figure turns out to be a malevolent manipulator who would not hesitate to kill him if necessary. In short, Chapter 2 will focus on a difficult question: which one is worse? An absent father or a lying father?

Notes

1 These experiences cover a wide range of negative situations in the family, such as physical abuse, emotional abuse, sexual abuse, substance abuse, physical neglect, emotional neglect, imprisonment of a family member, mental illness, parental loss, violence between parents/parental figures, etc.
2 Father absence due to divorce/separation or abandonment apparently had the most negative influence in the first two years of children regardless of their gender. Father absence due to death, however, affected boys aged 6–9 the worst.
3 Hollis specifically uses the term 'pseudo-fathers', indicating the bogus, fraudulent, insincere nature of these people.
4 Of course Roy is restricted in two different ways. Not just because he was wounded, but he also has been an officer in the armed services, an environment which would not allow sympathy and rapport beyond strictly defined situations.
5 Interestingly, Sagan's spectacular novel deals with another type of father hunger. This time, an astronomer daughter, deeply suffering from her father's early death when she was a child, travels across the galaxy to contact intelligent life forms which appear to her in a very familiar way.

References

Filmography

Ad Astra. (2019) Directed by J. Gray. USA.

Bibliography

Abraham, N. and Torok, M. (1994) *The Shell and the Kernel: Renewals of Psycho-analysis*. Volume I. Chicago: University of Chicago Press.

Abramovitch, S. (2022) 'Jeremy Strong knows what you think', available at: www.hollywoodreporter.com/movies/movie-features/jeremy-strong-armageddon-time-succession-1235228251.

American Psychiatric Association. (2013) *Diagnostic and Statistical Manual of Mental Disorders*. 5th ed. Arlington, VA: American Psychiatric Publishing.

Balcom, D. A. (1998) 'Absent fathers: Effects on abandoned sons', *The Journal of Men's Studies*, 6(3), 283–296.

Bartholomew, K. (1990) 'Avoidance of intimacy: An attachment perspective', *Journal of Social and Personal Relationships*, 7, 147–178.

Bellis M. A., Hughes, K., Leckenby, N., Jones, L., Baban, A., Kachaeva, M., Povilaitis, R., Pudule, I., Qirjako G., Ulukol, B., Raleva, M. and Terzic, N. (2014) 'Adverse childhood experiences and associations with health-harming behaviours in young adults: surveys in eight eastern European countries', *Bull World Health Organ*, 92, 641–655. http://dx.doi.org/10.2471/BLT.13.129247.

Biedermann, H. (1996a) 'Gates and Portals', in *The Wordsworth Dictionary of Symbolism*. Ware: Wordsworth Editions.

Biedermann, H. (1996b) 'Moon', in *The Wordsworth Dictionary of Symbolism*. Ware: Wordsworth Editions.

Biedermann, H. (1996c) 'Ape', in *The Wordsworth Dictionary of Symbolism*. Ware: Wordsworth Editions.

Biedermann, H. (1996d) 'Mars', in *The Wordsworth Dictionary of Symbolism*. Ware: Wordsworth Editions.

Biedermann, H. (1996e) 'Trident', in *The Wordsworth Dictionary of Symbolism*. Ware: Wordsworth Editions.

Blechman, E. A. (1982) 'Are children with one parent at psychological risk? A methodological review', *Journal of Marriage and Family*, 44(1), 179–195.

Brin, D. (1999) '"Star Wars" Despots vs. "Star Trek" Populists', *Salon*, 15 June, available at: www.salon.com/1999/06/15/brin_main/.

Brooks, X. (2019) 'Ad Astra review: Brad Pitt reaches the stars in superb space-opera with serious daddy issues', *The Guardian*, 29 August, available at: www.theguardian.com/film/2019/aug/29/ad-astra-review-brad-pitt-reaches-the-stars-in-superb-space-opera-with-serious-daddy-issues.

Byng-Hall, J. (1991) 'The application of attachment theory to understanding and treatment in family therapy', in C. Parkes, J. Stevenson-Hinde, and P. Marris (eds) *Attachment across the Life Cycle*. New York: Routledge, pp. 199–215.

Campbell, J. (1949) *The Hero with a Thousand Faces*. New York: Pantheon Books.

Campbell, W. K. and Foster, J. D. (2007) 'The narcissistic self: Background, an extended agency model, and ongoing controversies', in C. Sedikides and S. J. Spencer (eds) *The Self*. New York: Psychology Press, pp. 115–138.

Chevalier, J. and Gheerbrant, A. (1996a) 'Ship' in *The Penguin Dictionary of Symbols*. London: Penguin.

Chevalier, J. and Gheerbrant, A. (1996b) 'Moon, The (Planet)' in *The Penguin Dictionary of Symbols*. London: Penguin.

Chevalier, J. and Gheerbrant, A. (1996c) 'Monkey' in *The Penguin Dictionary of Symbols*. London: Penguin.

Chevalier, J. and Gheerbrant, A. (1996d) 'Ares (Mars)' in *The Penguin Dictionary of Symbols*. London: Penguin.

Chevalier, J. and Gheerbrant, A. (1996e) 'Neptune' in *The Penguin Dictionary of Symbols*. London: Penguin.

Corby, B., Shemmings, D. and Wilkins, D. (2012) *Child Abuse: An Evidence Base for Confident Practice*. Maidenhead: Open University Press.

Corneau, G. (1991) *Absent Fathers, Lost Sons: The Search for Masculine Identity*. Boston: Shambhala.

Cousineau, P. (ed.) (1990) *The Hero's Journey: Joseph Campbell on His Life and Work*. New York: Harper & Row.

Crocker, B. (2009) *The Children of Narcissus: Exploring the Development of Existential Trauma*. Pacifica Graduate Institute.

Daniel, B. (2015) 'Why have we made neglect so complicated? Taking a fresh look at noticing and helping the neglected child', *Child Abuse Review*, 24(2), 82–94.

Dundes, A. (ed.) (1984) *Sacred Narrative: Readings in the Theory of Myth*. Berkeley: University of California Press.

Felitti, V. J., Anda, R. F., Nordenberg, D., Williamson, D. F., Spitz, A. M., Edwards, V., Koss, M. P. and Marks, J. S. (1998) 'Relationship of childhood abuse and household dysfunction to many of the leading causes of death in adults: The adverse childhood experiences (ACE) study', *American Journal of Preventative Medicine*, 14 (4), 245–258.

Gleiberman, O. (2019) 'Film review: Ad Astra', available at: https://variety.com/2019/film/reviews/ad-astra-review-brad-pitt-tommy-lee-jones-1203317838/.

Greene, L. (1996) *The Astrological Neptune and the Quest for Redemption*. York Beach: Samuel Weiser.

Hanson, J. L., Adluru, N., Chung, M. K., Alexander, A. L., Davidson, R. J., and Pollak, S. D. (2013) 'Early Neglect Is Associated With Alterations in White Matter Integrity and Cognitive Functioning', *Child Development*, 84(5), 1566–1578.

Hillman, J. (1989) *Puer Papers*. Dallas: Spring Publications.

Hollis, J. (1994) *Under Saturn's Shadow: The Wounding and Healing of Men*. Toronto: Inner City Books.

Holmwood, M. (2023) *Traumatic Loss and Recovery in Jungian Studies and Cinema: Transdisciplinary Approaches in Grief Theory*. Abingdon: Routledge.

Horwath, J. (2007) *Neglect Identification and Assessment*. Basingstoke: Palgrave Macmillan.

Howe, D. (2005) *Child Abuse and Neglect Attachment, Development and Intervention*. London: Red Globe Press.

Jung, C. G. (1969) *The Collected Works of C. G. Jung, Volume 6: Psychological Types*. Princeton: Princeton University Press.

Jung, C. G. (1969) *The Collected Works of C. G. Jung, Volume 9 (Part 1): Archetypes and the Collective Unconscious*. Princeton: Princeton University Press.

Jung, C. G. (1969) *The Collected Works of C. G. Jung, Volume 9 (Part 2): Aion: Researches into the Phenomenology of the Self*. Princeton: Princeton University Press.

Jung, C. G. (1970) *The Collected Works of C. G. Jung, Volume 10: Civilization in Transition*. Princeton: Princeton University Press.

Jung, C. G. (1968) *The Collected Works of C. G. Jung, Volume 12: Psychology and Alchemy.* Princeton: Princeton University Press.

Jung, C. G. (1989) *Memories, Dreams, Reflections.* New York: Vintage Books.

Leeming, D. A. (1981) *Mythology: The Voyage of the Hero.* New York: Harper & Row.

Miller, J. D., Hoffman, B. J., Gaughan, E. T., Gentile, B., Maples, J. and Campbell, W. K. (2011) 'Grandiose and vulnerable narcissism: A nomological network analysis', *Journal of Personality*, 79, 1013–1042.

Monk, I. R. (2001) 'Adult Children of Covertly Narcissistic Families: A Look at Their Romantic Relationships'. Thesis, University of British Columbia. https://doi.org/10.14288/1.0053880.

Morrison, A. P. (1986) 'Introduction', in A. P. Morrison (ed.) *Essential Papers on Narcissism.* New York: New York University Press, pp. 1–12.

Radford, L.*et al.* (2011) *Child Abuse and Neglect in the UK Today.* London: NSPCC. Available at: https://learning.nspcc.org.uk/research-resources/pre-2013/child-abuse-neglect-uk-today.

Reuben, A., Moffitt, T. E., Caspi, A., Belsky, D. W., Harrington, H., Schroeder, F., Hogan, S., Ramrakha, S., Poulton, R. and Danese, A. (2016) 'Lest we forget: Comparing retrospective and prospective assessments of adverse childhood experiences in the prediction of adult health', *The Journal of Child Psychology and Psychiatry*, 57(10), 1103–1112. https://doi.org/10.1111/jcpp.12621.

Ronnberg, A. and Martin, K. (eds) (2010) 'Ape/monkey', in *The Book of Symbols: Reflections on Archetypal Images.* Cologne: Taschen.

Sagan, C. (1986) *Contact.* London: Arrow Books.

Santrock, J. W. (1972) 'Relation of Type and Onset of Father Absence to Cognitive Development', *Child Development*, 43(2), 455–469.

Schwartz, S. E. (2021) *The Absent Father Effect on Daughters: Father Desire, Father Wounds.* Abingdon: Routledge.

Segal, R. A. (1984) 'Joseph Campbell's theory of myth', in A. Dundes (ed.) *Sacred Narrative: Readings in the Theory of Myth.* Berkeley: University of California Press, pp. 256–269.

Seligman, E. (1985) 'The half-alive ones', in A. Samuels (ed.) *The Father: Contemporary Jungian Perspectives.* London: Free Association Books, pp. 69–94.

Seligman, E. (2018) *The Half-Alive Ones: Clinical Papers on Analytical Psychology in a Changing World.* Abingdon: Routledge.

Vogler, C. (2007) *The Writer's Journey: Mythic Structure for Writers.* Los Angeles: Michael Wiese Productions.

Chapter 2

The manipulator

While the absence of a father can be detrimental to a child's development, the presence of one can be even worse. This is particularly the case when that father, or father figure, is loving, caring and supportive with a dark, ulterior motive. *Partisan*, a 2015 Australian film directed by Ariel Kleiman, presents a challenging case of a father–child relationship, focusing on power imbalance and the slow but steadily growing resistance towards this disparity.

Kleiman wrote the screenplay with his girlfriend Sarah Cyngler. After reading about real-life child assassins in Colombia (Variety, 2015), he developed his part fairy tale and part nightmarish vision of a timeless battle between an oppressive and manipulative patriarch and his adopted offspring. The film premiered at the Sundance Film Festival in 2015 and it is Kleiman's first full-length feature as a director. Shot in Georgia and Australia, the film was nominated for the Grand Jury Prize at Sundance and won the World Cinema Cinematography Award.

Partisan depicts a heart-wrenching, thought-provoking drama where scenes of safe, happy, and nurtured childhood are interwoven with carefully calculated and heartlessly executed murder scenes. This sharp contrast becomes the core of the narrative where love turns into manipulation, safety involves ignorance or indifference, and death becomes a game children play with gay abandon. As the increasingly disturbing tale reaches its unavoidable conclusion, the overwhelming feeling of sadness is replaced with a tiny spark of hope, a hope for a different future where the perpetual and generational pattern of conflict between fathers and sons might cease and be replaced with something they both deserve.

In order to present Kleiman's story in detail, I will examine its content in three parts. The first part will look at the chain of events depicted in the film and the recurring symbols that contribute to this narrative. The second part will investigate the concept of manipulation and how it can poison parent–child bonding. The third part will explore the Jungian connections further for an interconnected reading of this tale of love, loss, and violence.

DOI: 10.4324/9781003394488-2

Babies and chains: symbols of innocence and obedience

While the film seems to tell the tale of a patriarch, it is mainly told through the eyes, experiences, and the keen observations of a child named Alexander (Jeremy Chabriel) who is very quickly established as the main protagonist. The story is based on how Gregori (Vincent Cassel) runs and manages a secret community close to a decaying town, cut off from the outside world and only accessible through a maze of tunnels. This community is made up of women and their children who are handpicked by Gregori due to their dire circumstances. It is suggested that Gregori regularly visits maternal wards and finds women who have recently given birth but have no relatives or income to support themselves. With his charm and compassion, Gregori invites these women to his community and 'unofficially adopts' their babies as the nurturing, protecting father figure.

This is how the baby Alexander (Charlotte Miller) and his mother Susanna (Florence Mezzara) end up at Gregori's compound at the beginning of the film. Eleven years later, now with other women and children around, Gregori is the only adult male of the community, carefully portrayed as the charismatic and powerful man who is depicted like the embodiment of a polygamist's dream. Gregori is not only responsible for the provisions, education, and the protection of this community but also the groomer of a group of child assassins which Alexander is a part of. By using these innocent-looking but deadly children, Gregori plans and orchestrates the assignments which Uncle Charlie (Frank Moylan) pays for in cash and brings presents for children. This surreal and bloody set-up starts going off the rails after Leo (Alex Balaganskiy) and his mother Rosa (Rosa Voto) join the community. As a very clever and neurodiverse child, Leo starts correcting Gregori's comments and refuses to follow his orders, including eating chicken. Gregori does not take this defiant attitude lightly, and after an uneasy confrontation Leo and his mother disappear. Having lost his friend so suddenly, Alexander quietly begins to question Gregori's motives and everything he taught him. After Susanna gives birth to his brother Tobias (Evie Baker/Levi Watts) and tells Alexander about babies and innocence, he becomes more and more torn between trust and mistrust as his mother does not seem to mind the fact that he is a child assassin. Following his last assassination, he picks up Tobias and tries to run away only to be confronted by Gregori. During this tense finale, Gregori tells Alexander that he is just a child, and he would never survive without him. The film ends with Alexander pointing his gun at Gregori after putting earplugs on Tobias for protection.

Partisan, while it explores complicated and opposing concepts like protection and danger, love and deceit, life and death in fictional parent–child relationships, finds its starting point and foundation in real life. The use of children as hitmen is indeed common in Colombia, and this horrible and cruel tradition has been going on for at least 20 years. These child assassins are called *sicarios*,[1] and as Delgado (2010) notes, many sicarios in Medellín are underage blood relatives of the mafia members who were a part of Pablo Escobar's Cartel in the 1980s and 1990s. Only in 2009, they were responsible for over 6000 murders (ibid.) and their age at the time of their first murder can be as young as 13. According to Charles (2021), the deadly tasks of these children are not restricted to only being hitmen. They can also be soldiers, getaway drivers, explosive/landmine experts, cocaine laboratory workers, or drug dealers/mules. Children coming from poor and marginalised communities, having no access to educational opportunities, are snapped up by grooming gangs because they are easy and cheap to recruit, and security forces find it hard to detect them due to their age and innocent looks. Each successful murder payment they receive can range from US$97 to US$2,000, as opposed to hiring a professional for US$24,000 (Delgado, 2010). Motorcycle is the most common vehicle used during each assignment. One child becomes the driver while the second child as the main shooter easily focuses on the target without distraction.[2]

These child assassins are the products of a vicious circle where the chances of a better family life are denied due to poverty, ineffective social welfare systems, and a lack of parental employment. Therefore, they feel obliged to do something to support their families. While some of them are forced by gangs to carry out these tasks, some of them voluntarily join in because crime appears as the only job opportunity. Their only two ways out of this life seem to be either dying or, if they are lucky, being helped by a sympathetic gang member in finding a foster family elsewhere and never coming back (Charles, 2021). Either way, they have an isolated, violent, and frequently a very short life.[3] Even when they leave the violence behind and start a new life, they are faced with an ongoing rejection and stigma which restricts their reintegration to society (Denov and Marchand, 2014).

Kleiman builds his narrative based on this isolation and violence, and ties the film's opening scene, showing Gregori on his own away from the crumbling and shabby town, with the closing scene where his death is imminent. Alexander's tragic journey follows a parallel pattern in the film. Even though he thinks he is in a loving, safe, and nurturing environment at the beginning, he slowly realises that it is only sustainable through his and the other children's violent acts which, as the film progresses, start to alienate him, and make him feel isolated. Moreover, Alexander finds his way out of this life by standing up to a manipulative and ruthless father figure (rather than being destroyed by him) which makes the film even more interesting from a pedagogical perspective.

Kleiman opens the film with a five-minute prologue: Gregori is carrying a heavy wooden beam on his shoulder with different types of table legs tied to the beam. He walks away from the town, heading towards his compound, and drags the beam inside with great effort. In the next scene, Kleiman diligently shows the compound's bare interior. From many used mattresses stacked on top of each other to old cups, plates, and chandeliers standing by the corner, it is clear that Gregori is up to something as the camera shows a handgun resting next to a bag full of cash. Carefully framed with his topless and muscular back in focus, he fixes and lifts a heavy table with a marble top, out of breath and groaning as the camera highlights his power, virility, and ability to build a new environment for himself and others. As a contrast to these two scenes, the following scene takes place at a maternity ward. Gregori walks around in an old hospital building with cracked walls, dirty sinks, and rusty bed frames. The camera shifts to Susanna, who is lying in her bed with a bruised lip (indicating physical violence) and gazing into the distance with sad eyes. Other mothers in the ward have visitors but she does not. Gregori notices her loneliness, walks in, and kindly asks if he can sit down. He puts his boutonnière in the empty vase next to Susanna and explains how that empty vase helped him notice her. In this scene, he meets the baby Alexander as well, with the softness and charm of a gentle, compassionate father who appears like a saviour to both. As Susanna looks impressed with this type of kindness, Gregori's plans are set in motion.

This prologue appears before the film's title is shown on the screen and is key to understand Gregori's character, motivation, and behaviour which follow a strict pattern without deviation all through the story. He is depicted as a resourceful, physically able man who is creating a living space from scratch, using old and used materials people discarded. His pistols (the second one appears after he lifts the marble table) imply his preferred way of offence/protection. His alluring and tender appearance at the maternity ward, even though it sweeps Susanna off her feet then and there, shows he is not only predatory but also cunning and manipulative as he hand-picks her due to her visible vulnerability. Kleiman plays with this concept of a father figure who has power, who can provide and protect, but also who can deceive, control and exploit with precision all throughout the film.

From this point onwards, the story makes a forward jump in time, and it is revealed that, after 11 years, Gregori's community has grown and prospered, with seven women and their children now living with him. Kleiman, however, specifically ties the beginning and the ending of *Partisan* with the camera focusing on two different babies: Alexander and Tobias. In other words, he uses the image of a baby to convey an intricate and interconnected narrative that runs throughout the film.

Babies, infants, and in general children are the eternal and recurring symbols of innocence, simplicity and purity, hope, optimism and sometimes the promise of a better future, widely used in the arts and religious/sacred texts worldwide. Chevalier and Gheerbrant (1996a) also mention the famous Taoist philosopher Zhuang Zhou and his writings about children, and how they are natural and unforced, gentle and non-aggressive, and how they are spontaneous, frank and direct as opposed to adults who can easily be cunning, calculative and insidious. They also mention the Hindu term *bālya* which is comparable to the state of innocent obedience of Adam and Eve in the Garden of Eden before the Fall. Christian tradition continued this state of uncorruptedness and purity specifically in the depiction of angels as they have been repeatedly portrayed as babies or children with wings, white and glowing. Moreover, in the Gospel of Matthew (chapter 18, verse 3), it is made clear that the kingdom of heaven will not be accessible unless people change and become like little children, indicating a necessary inner transformation, a pre-requisite to receive the grace of God.

The film plays on this thread of innocence and evil coming together in a circular narrative. Alexander, as a baby, comes into the world in a pure and peaceful state, completely unaware of the violence and murders that await him. He also becomes the key to secure Susanna's future in Gregori's compound, away from poverty, physically safe and looked after. When Tobias is born, Alexander, now nearly 12, is fascinated by the innocent vulnerability of his baby brother, and vows to protect him. He discovers that Gregori is lying, and Susanna, instead of protecting him and Tobias as their mother from Gregori and future assassination assignments, is not willing to go against Gregori for the fear of being kicked out, or worse, killed. Therefore, she appears as the supporter of Gregori's lifestyle and criminal organisation by staying silent, obedient, but as culpable as him.

It is important to note that Susanna is not the only woman who contributes to the corruption of the children and assists Gregori in creating child assassins. During the killing practice scene (19:35), Kleiman depicts an interaction between another woman and a boy living in the compound. The boy is learning how to shoot and kill, and the woman is acting as an unsuspecting target. Even though a paintball gun is used during this practice, it is clear that all the women are fully aware of what Gregori is doing, and how he earns money. In other words, they are actively participating in this evil scheme where these children are robbed of their innocence.

This loss of innocence is probably best symbolised by the Eve statue which is the central feature of the fountain in the film. Depicting a half-naked woman with a big snake on her shoulders, this statue undeniably alludes to the Garden of Eden myth. While the Abrahamic religions differ in their perspectives regarding the events that led to Adam and Eve being sent down to Earth, Christian tradition sees Eve as the original sinner who (with the encouragement of the serpent) not only gave into temptation and ate the forbidden fruit of knowledge, but also offered it to Adam and corrupted him as well. It is important to remember that Eve was also the mother of Cain and Abel and, through this offspring, linked to the first murder. From being a seducer to giving birth to a murderer, Eve appears as an archetypal bridge between creation and destruction.

Kleiman develops his parallel narrative on this dark side of female influence and motherhood further by highlighting the chicken/hen symbol in his film. Chickens first appear in the film when they are killed by two women in the compound (52:16) while they are teaching Rosa how to do it. Their instructions are quite specific. Apparently, holding chickens upside down has a hypnotic effect on them, and they become calm and confused, which makes things easier before one swiftly chops their heads off. Unfortunately, Leo also sees this killing, gets extremely disturbed as a neurodiverse child, and decides to protect the chickens from anyone and everyone (including Gregori) by sitting in the pen day and night. Leo's unflinching determination as a little boy sets in motion the things that unravel the seemingly safe and loving life in the compound.

Hens, as adult female chickens, have been regarded completely different compared to roosters. A symbol of classic devoted motherhood, hens are vigilant, and they protect their defenceless offspring from intruders and the elements. However, they are also considered unintelligent, confused, and likely to panic easily (Biedermann, 1996b; Ronnberg and Martin, 2010a). Biedermann (1996b) also quotes Aeppli (1960) and his Jungian dream interpretation of hens, describing them as witless, gullible creatures which are vulnerable to outside influence.

Leo's rebellious behaviour in the henhouse is met with compassion from other women. They bring blankets and electric heaters to keep him warm during the night. The following morning, however, Gregori tells everyone how heartbreaking it was to find them both gone (61:12). As women and children gasp and express concern about their departure, it becomes clear that they believe Gregori whole-heartedly. This lack of suspicion is also highlighted by Alexander's shocked face and tears in his eyes. He knows Gregori is lying. This is due to the short and secret conversation he had with Leo during the night when Leo told him that Gregori would be taking him to get Tangier feathers in the morning, something he really liked. During this conversation Leo also asks Alexander to take care of the chickens while he is away, indicating his wish to return.

Gregori does not mention anything about this trip in his announcement. He just rambles about how Leo was a disturbed boy and how much he hopes Rosa does not get lost while trying to find Leo in the tunnels. Kleiman's camera focuses on two faces during this scene: Gregori and Alexander. As Gregori embellishes his lies about Leo, Alexander keeps on looking at him with infinite sadness, probably realising for the first time that the man he loved and killed for can be equally deceptive and murderous when his authority is challenged, and the women in the compound are unable to see the real Gregori, just like hypnotised hens held upside down.

The remaining chickens that were bequeathed to Alexander reappear during the lunch scene (65:01), but this time all dead and roasted, and they trigger the violent scene between Gregori and Alexander. When Alexander refuses to eat them, Gregori starts shouting and aggressively force-feeds him. Apart from no incoming help from any of the women including Susanna to stop Gregori, the roasted chickens also symbolise Gregori's visible dominance over and disguised menace to all of them. It is a clear warning that they will be butchered and thrown away if they dare to rebel like Leo.

This unquestioning and total obedience is probably best symbolised by the golden chain in the film. Given by Gregori as a present during Alexander's eleventh birthday, it is shown again around Alexander's neck after Leo is gone (63:53). It reappears on Alexander's twelfth birthday (73:55). However, this time there is a big difference. When Susanna asks Alexander why he is not wearing his necklace, he answers by saying it is stupid, indicating the loss of its meaning and value for him.

A necklace can generally be any type of accessory (chain, band, cord, beads or jewels) worn around the neck. Fashionable or not, it generally has a circular shape and is associated with the notion of linking. Apart from its additional visual connections to ties and collars, chain symbolises a bond, an association between the person who wears it and whoever (person, group, or organisation) has given or asked/forced them to wear it. Derived from *catēna*, 'fetter' in Latin, chain suggests hauling, supporting, confining, domestic animals, shackles, bondage, prison, slavery, and defeat.

Biedermann (1996a) points out the varying symbology of chains, both in the iconography of the devil, defeated after the Last Judgment and thrown into the abyss in chains, and the chain of Saint Peter which he was released from by an angel. In Greek mythology, the famous punishment given by Zeus results in Prometheus being chained to a rock and his liver eaten daily by an eagle. Linking vanquishment and liberation, chain evokes the unbreakable bond between cause and effect, repeated in a seemingly endless circular pattern. Chevalier and Gheerbrant (1996b) also note the mythical judge Morann in Celtic myths, whose necklace would tighten around his neck if his verdict was unjust and go loose if he was fair. This interconnectedness makes the chain symbol figuratively connect two diametrically opposed states together: intimacy and support[4] versus subjugation and defeat.

Kleiman depicts these states, and the way Alexander deals with them quite frankly. When he wears the golden chain for the first time during his birthday, he is smiling, proud, feeling accepted and loved by everyone in the compound, but specifically by the only father figure in his life. Therefore, that chain becomes a symbol of his link both to this secret community and to Gregori. One full year later, after witnessing Leo's defiance and its consequences, being subjected to Gregori's violence, and realising that his mother has no intention to prevent Tobias from becoming another child assassin, that chain becomes the very symbol of subjugation and oppression, a stupid piece of jewellery which reminds him of Gregori's sweet lies to keep everyone under his control. That is why he takes Tobias with him and runs away, making sure he saves an innocent baby, his own brother from a blood-splattered future, a future Tobias is destined to have if he stays with Gregori. By liberating both of them, he makes sure he breaks the chain, the circular pattern of violence which every baby and every child is expected, if not forced, to be a part of.

Partisan builds its story on a harrowing reality of this world where children are taught to harm, trained to kill. Instead of spending their early years in the comfort and safety of their own home, they are instructed to face the world in the most lethal way possible. Failed soldiers of fortune, they are victims of adverse circumstances. Maybe this is why Kleiman highlights the toxicity of power through Gregori's character. As Ramji (2015) notes, not every authority figure has the best intentions, and not every haven is a place of safety. Gregori, as the seemingly benevolent father figure to all the children in the film, not only controls and influences them, but also exploits their naïveté in the worst possible way. The next section will look at this rather artful but certainly wicked and sinister skill of psychological domination.

He is lying: manipulation and exploitation

In the French DVD edition of the film, released by Arp Sélection, there is a short interview with the director. In this interview, Kleiman expands on his inspiration for the film. He says that, apart from the New York Times article on child assassins in Colombia, he also saw Carlos Saura's film *Cría Cuervos* (1976). The film's title, based on the Spanish proverb 'Cría cuervos y te sacarán los ojos', means 'raising ravens' and refers to the proverb's full meaning: 'If you raise ravens, they will claw your eyes out'. This rather scathing expression covers a range of situations including unlucky parenting, rebellious youth, and how even good deeds can lead to disastrous outcomes. Kleiman mentions this proverb within the context of how he sees Gregori. As the director and co-scriptwriter, he says he ultimately has empathy for Gregori as he finds him human and paternal despite his horrendous acts.

It is quite surprising (if not unsettling) to hear about the director's sympathetic, almost loving remarks about a lying, deceiving and exploitative character which the film's narrative is exposing comprehensively. On the one hand, Gregori is very comfortable in being the gentle, playful, and extremely likeable father figure to a group of fatherless children. He is not only affectionate towards them but also towards their mothers. His tender and caring behaviour when he finds Susanna and Alexander at the hospital during the prologue, gradually morphs into a poly-amorous interaction with other women which is clearly visible during the adult party scene (41:00). He is never hostile or violent towards any of them in the film. In return, the women simply adore this saviour who has snatched them up from the hostile environment they were once in, do not doubt or question his authority once, and they see no problem in sharing him sexually with each other. It is quite apparent that in the eyes of these vulnerable and powerless women Gregori is the best possible father figure, provider, educator, and protector.

Yet, this seemingly wonderful man is not only an efficient killer, but also a rather delicate tyrant who drops his mask of compassion swiftly when his authority is questioned or openly challenged. He does not hesitate to get rid of Leo as soon as he realises that Leo will continue to point out any mistakes in his actions or any lies in his words. When Alexander refuses to eat chicken, Gregori sees this as an echo of Leo's single-minded behaviour and resorts to violence to re-establish his dominance. But of course, what makes Gregori so scary and unforgivable is his malignant talent in distorting every comment, fact, and situation in order to protect his lifestyle and the compound he built from scratch. This twisting and misrepresenting of reality is simply and notoriously known as manipulation.

Psychological/emotional manipulation is a broad subject, and the manipulation techniques people use in close or professional relationships can vary. Feigning love and faking empathy, aggression, emotional blackmail, denial, flattery, love-bombing, silent treatment, even sarcasm and positive reinforcement can be employed in order to make people think and behave in a certain way. These maladaptive behaviours are efforts to escape accountability and deflect responsibility, and when people engage in these behaviours with intent and forethought, they become toxic.

While some scholars use the term psychological manipulation, others prefer emotional manipulation, and these two terms overlap due to the nature of their outcome. When a manipulative person tries to obtain power over someone else through coercive, unethical, dishonest, and exploitative means, the result is mental distortion/confusion and inconspicuous abuse of feelings which push that person towards thoughts and actions they would not normally agree with. As Geis (1970) noted, for a manipulator to successfully manipulate others, they would have to be willing, have the ability, and the belief (or the confidence) that others can be manipulated. Emotional intelligence (EI), which is the capacity to perceive, identify, and understand emotions, and utilise this information to make decisions (Salovey and Mayer, 1990), becomes a dark power when it is specifically and strategically used to gain personal advantage or reward. Research into EI has shown that tactics such as situation-based, emotion-specific, and intentional expressions can assist self-serving actions (Kilduff et al., 2010), and these tactics form the basis of manipulative behaviours of Machiavellians, narcissists, and psychopaths (Davis and Nichols, 2016).

Maybe named a bit dramatically, the term 'the dark triad' (Paulhus and Williams, 2002) refers to this three-way constellation of harmful personality traits where Machiavellianism (favouring expediency over ethics, amorality), narcissism (sense of entitlement, inflated perception of self-worth and importance), and psychopathy (insensitive and cruel disregard for others, absence of empathy, rash behaviour) come together and create the fertile ground for emotional manipulation. While high levels of psychopathy and EI indicate strong emotional manipulation capacity for people regardless of their gender, research shows that males not only engage in more emotional manipulation compared to females but also self-disclose it more freely (Grieve and Mahar, 2010; Bacon and Regan, 2016; Grieve et al., 2018). This interesting frequency of self-disclosure can be interpreted as an expression of success in dominating others.

Coined by Connell (1987, 2000), hegemonic masculinity is the concept commonly used to refer to men's dominant social roles and the power dynamics these roles produce and perpetuate in society. In other words, it is the stereotypical notion of an unattainable maximum maleness which not only demands the domination of women and other gender identities (gay, trans, non-binary, etc.) which are deemed to be subservient, less important, or simply inferior to a proper/real man, but also creates a hierarchy of men. Therefore, misogyny, homophobia/transphobia, aggressive competitiveness, degradation of anything feminine, fear of being vulnerable or being perceived as such are all components of this idealised, fetishised, and rather mythical maleness.[5] Consequently, emotional manipulation becomes a remarkable tool to establish and perpetuate domination, and to advance the narrative of being a triumphant 'alpha male'. As Waddell et al. (2020) argue, hegemonic masculinity and dark personality traits (such as Machiavellianism) seem to share common ground which brings dominance and deception together.

In order to establish and sustain dominance, is deception necessary? While the real-life answer to this question is open to debate, the fictional narrative of *Partisan* delivers a straightforward 'yes' via Gregori's craftiness. His dark personality traits, his manipulation, and his cruelty are visible in four key scenes: the group meeting scene after Rosa and Leo's arrival (14:10); the karaoke scene (23:10) which then leads into Gregori's 'the way of the world speech' scene (29:12); and the final confrontation scene of Gregori and Alexander (84:09).

Right after Gregori brings Rosa and Leo to the compound, the adults have a meeting. The children and Rosa are not present. While the women talk about the newcomers, one of them wonders if they have room to accommodate Rosa and her two children. Susanna immediately answers by saying they can always make room, openly supporting Gregori's decision to bring in a new woman for his harem and a new potential killer for his team of child assassins. Gregori then tells how his conversation went with Rosa at the hospital, how Rosa was in such a desperate state and that she told him she felt like a caught fish flapping on a chopping board, losing a battle against the absence of water and the impending blade. This colourful and evocative language is of course deliberate. Gregori is deliberately making all the women remember their helpless state before they met him, and how he gave them (and their babies) a safe place and a new life, making sure that not only Rosa is not treated badly or excluded by the group, but also his saviour status is reinforced. He even suggests that this arrangement can be temporary if Rosa decides to leave after she gets better, as if she has an alternative path for survival. In other words, he uses these women's history and experience of hopelessness and vulnerability against them so that they do not question his motives and choices, and exploits their empathy so that he can have sex with

Rosa freely (which is heavily suggested in the next scene where Rosa comes out of the shower wrapped in a towel with wet hair, and a naked Gregori, in bed, blows her a kiss; 15:52).

Gregori's impressive metaphors and figurative language do not stop here. He organises a special karaoke night in order to celebrate the most efficient killer of the week (presented as the child with the highest number of gold stars on the board). Ariana (Anastasia Prystay) and Alexander come jointly at the top and they share a duet called 'The Hardest Thing to Do'.[6] This singalong with a killer 80s synthetic vibe, chosen specifically by Gregori, has curious lines in terms of adding context to the narrative. The song talks about a trap, set up for two people, and mentions how telling the truth can be the hardest thing to do. Apart from foreshadowing the final scene of the film where Alexander sets up a trap for Gregori, it also underlines the difficulty of honest discussions which never take place in the film, especially between adults. What makes this karaoke scene crucial in terms of Gregori's manipulation, however, is that he twists the horrible act of killing somebody (or rather making a child kill somebody) into an achievement which deserves public praise and celebration. As Ariana and Alexander sing the song together on the colourful stage rather cheerlessly and in a serious manner, the camera pans over the faces of other children who watch these two successful killers in awe and admiration, transfixed and enchanted, probably wishing to be on that stage one day. In other words, Gregori skilfully corrupts these children's innocence and humanity and tries to make sure that these children feel pride and joy when they kill somebody (instead of guilt or regret) as their actions will be encouraged, supported, celebrated, and rewarded by him and their mothers openly.

After all the adults clap and cheer for Ariana's and Alexander's performance, Gregori takes Alexander to the schooling area of the compound and empties his backpack in front of him. Revealing he is aware of the little plastic toys Alexander secretly collected on his way back from his assignments, he gently asks him not to hide anything from him. He then tells Alexander how he was smitten with his mother's perfume after she died, and one day he accidentally burned his arm, discovering that perfumes are flammable. As he describes how his arm was burning, he also tells that nobody came for help, and how he would always be there for Alexander, not only protecting him from all the evils of the world but also teaching him how to protect himself, Susanna, and Tobias. It is not known whether this story is true, and while it may be acceptable to teach children about dangerous people and situations they might face, what Gregori is doing here is carefully implanting in Alexander a sense of suspicion and mistrust of other people, insecurity and fear, presenting himself as the ultimate and infallible protector, and reinforcing the narrative that Alexander's murders, now or in the future, are permissible.

This is why this short scene foreshadows the final confrontation between the man and the boy at the end of the film. As the narrative builds up to this confrontation, Alexander tries to warn his mother about him (69:55). While she is breastfeeding and burping Tobias, Susanna says babies can sense energies other people do not notice, and therefore it is important not to have negative people around babies, inadvertently fuelling Alexander's mistrust. But when Alexander asks if she thinks Gregori is lying, she suddenly gets very angry, avoids answering the question, and leaves Alexander with the baby, looking confused and rejected. Plus, just before Alexander's last assignment Gregori gives him a hug, telling him how they want to give the children a life they did not have so that they can learn how to fight back in an ugly, dangerous world. Alexander carefully points out the fact that Gregori did not like Leo fighting back. With disdain, Gregori says Leo's fight for the chickens was trivial, and asks the most crucial question of the film: if Alexander prefers to hit a man first or be hit by him (77:15). Alexander's reply, now feeling abandoned by his mother as well, is curt and without hesitation. He says he would hit first, meaning he would not be tricked like Leo.

Following his last murder which shows that he is increasingly hesitant and uncomfortable with being a killer, Alexander comes back into the compound, bleeding. He decisively picks up Tobias and leaves. Gregori runs after him with bandages and finds Alexander sitting in one of the tunnels, looking tearful, holding Tobias in his arms. When Gregori insists on taking them back, Alexander picks up his pistol and aims at Gregori. He repeats what his mother had told him earlier, that babies can sense bad energies. This is when Gregori's caring father figure mask slips. With contempt, condescension, and visible irritation, he says to Alexander that he is just a little child, nothing more, and he knows how to hold a gun only because he was taught by him.

In this tense finale, Alexander has tears in his eyes, but he is calm. Having revealed the real, ugly face underneath the manipulator, his hand does not shake. There is almost a serene, satisfied expression on his face, now completely sure he is doing the right thing. The film ends with the powerful image of Alexander, slowly rocking Tobias in his arms (88:26). Tobias has plugs in his ears, indicating Alexander's wish to protect them from the impending shotgun noise. The director does not show the actual murder before the credits. Instead, the camera focuses on Tobias, the baby without a chain, the uncorrupted innocence, the hope, the way out of this violent circle of dominance that kills men and his offspring in every generation.

As mentioned earlier, Kleiman sees the whole story, from its gentle beginning at the hospital to its foreboding end in the tunnels, as an example of an intergenerational discord, an unavoidable parent–child conflict, and contextually compares it to an animal (raven) being violent towards its owner (clawing their eyes out). By using this analogy, he seems to suggest that Alexander is somewhat owned by Gregori, that he is being ungrateful for everything Gregori has done for him, and he seems to ignore the main premise of the film where children are mistreated and victimised in different ways by both parents/parental figures, and where at least one child is taking a stand against this situation by using the same method he has been taught.

Janoff-Bulman (1992) notes that children growing up in a safe environment where care givers are positive and loving form the belief that people are trustworthy, the world is civilised and peaceful, and life is inherently meaningful. When that environment includes habitual violence, cruelty and neglect, children are traumatised. Due to this experience, their outlook on life, future expectations, regulation of adverse emotions are affected negatively, blighting their adult lives (Fitzgerald, 1988; Berntsen and Rubin, 2006). They are unable to trust other people, and consequently, unable to form and maintain deep and meaningful relationships. This detrimental effect of child abuse is explored further in Chapter Three.

Psychological/emotional manipulation is a form of abuse by stealth. Therefore, Alexander's final act of rescuing himself and Tobias from a manipulative environment by killing the manipulator cannot be likened to a child being ungrateful for any reason. It is rather a courageous achievement which has the potential to deliver a monumental shift in his psyche and his relationship with the world when he grows up. The next section will look at his choice and the environment he leaves behind from a Jungian perspective.

Masks, tricks, and rebellion: start of a new cycle

In Weiner and Gallo-Silver's (2019) alphabetised list of Jungian archetypes, a rather curious entry exists: 'devious cat'. While it is not possible to find a section dedicated to an archetype called 'devious cat' in Jung's *Collected Works*, Jung did write about cats and kittens: for example, in relation to dreams (CW 1, para. 253); word association (CW 2, para. 11; CW 2, para. 432; CW 2, para. 605); and preservation of species (CW 4, para. 235). Especially in his experiments in word association, his subjects connect the word 'cat' with sneakiness and being false. This is a rather common phenomenon. As Ronnberg and Martin (2010b) note, Christianity links cats with the disruptive qualities of women who are not obedient, modest, or moral, qualities also associated with the devil. These negative descriptions (also common in other cultures) about an animal which has night vision and can hunt in darkness as a predator have the potential to classify 'devious cat' as a derivative/variant archetype.

Hannah (2006), who was a student and a friend of Jung and who gave lectures on the archetypal symbolism of animals, associates cats with coziness, rage, independence, self-reliance, and false nature. Their unpredictable and independent behaviour as well as their ability to charm human beings are probably some of the reasons behind the word 'devious' which gives this archetype its main substance, suggesting a skilful use of secret and dishonest tactics to achieve goals.

This intentional dishonesty while appearing amiable and good-natured shares characteristics with three other Jungian archetypes: persona, shadow, and trickster. As the social mask people put on, persona is not inherently deceptive or hypocritical (Samuels et al., 2005). However, as it functions as the shop window which displays the products and valuables (meaning, it is the visible face of professional conduct, achievements, abilities, titles, and even gender identity), it dictates the narrative around and the perception of a specific role in public, such as surgeon, manager, father etc. Therefore, the real person underneath this social mask can be completely different to the face shown to the world. In Jung's words, persona hides the true character of the individual (CW 7, para. 305). One of the frequent examples of this duplicity is the double life of married heterosexual men who have children, and who not only exhibit a picture-perfect family life and defend religious values but also engage in homosexual extra-marital affairs in secret which conflict with the values and the image they advocate (Shapiro, 2012).

Defined by Jung as the darker side of personality (CW 11, para. 131), shadow is the totality of unpleasant, negative, flawed, inferior, and sometimes primitive and animalistic qualities one wants to ignore, hide, and repress. The less one is aware of their shadow, or the more the individual tries to hide it, the stronger it gets, and the tension, the chasm between the positive and the negative sides of personality grows. Therefore, the individual's conscious repression of their shadow can lead to intentionally deceptive and devious behaviour.

This two-facedness is probably best exemplified by another Jungian archetype: the trickster. Described as the combination of both a beast and a god-like being (CW 9i, para. 472), the trickster embodies a volatile, unpredictable, and conflicting nature. The Norse god Loki or the Greek deity Hermes, both known for their mischievous and cunning acts, are two frequently used examples for this archetype's intrinsically mercurial behaviour which upsets the current order and triggers revolutionary changes. Because the trickster follows his own agenda and he enjoys pranks, annoyance, or harm, he not only indicates a dubious area between good and bad but can also demonstrate a rather detached, insensitive, and irresponsible character.

While Jung defines the trickster archetype as a collective shadow character (CW 9i, para. 484), he also mentions that it is actually a parallel of the individual shadow (CW 9i, para. 485). Meaning, the individual and the collective mirror each other, feed off of each other, and they are simultaneously coexisting. In *Partisan*'s savage universe, the cruelty, the deception, and the unfairness of the outside world which Gregori keeps mentioning to justify his actions exist, because these outside realities are the parallels, the reflections, and in many ways, the extensions of his shadow. He morphs children's shooting practices into cheerful games. He grooms and uses the children as assassins, and he dresses it up as them helping him clean the outside world, making it better and less unfair. His secret compound which he argues he built to save the women and children from this cruel world is where his inner shadow dwells, as cruel, as deceptive, and as unfair as the outside world he describes.

As mentioned in the previous section, the dark triad plays an important role in emotional manipulation. While Machiavellianism, narcissism, and psychopathy may not directly correspond to the trickster, persona, or shadow, the fundamental behavioural and psychological patterns represented in these archetypes share common ground with emotional manipulation. Especially when it comes to psychopathy, Jung's position is quite clear. He says that it is not possible to find the majority of psychopaths in asylums (CW 10, para. 477), because they are considered to be within the range of being 'acceptable' (he uses the word 'normal'), meaning the nature and the severity of their psychopathic behaviour can vary, and they can blend in very easily without being spotted or diagnosed.[7] This means these people can be one's teacher, employer, neighbour, partner, or even father, and their manipulative behaviour, callousness, irresponsibility, and grandiose sense of self-worth can cause psychological (and in some cases physical) damage.

Is there a way to avoid or stop being manipulated? While many people might answer this question differently, Kleiman provides his solution by showing Alexander pointing his gun at Gregori. In other words, the damage caused by Gregori's dishonesty and cruelty is counterbalanced by Alexander's destructiveness, a lethal deed he has been carefully and repeatedly taught, a violent act he has been encouraged to commit. Of course, the irony here is that, Alexander, as a good student and a protégé, is strictly following the rules Gregori has set for him: hitting a man first rather than being hit by him.

Gregori's demise, or simply the reversal of fortune, is also linked to the trickster archetype. As Samuels et al. (2005) note, the trickster is the symbol of predisposition to enantiodromia. Jung defines enantiodromia as the universal law that governs every life cycle, and this law states that everything eventually and inevitably turns into its opposite (CW 6, para. 708). In the film, Gregori's sanctuary for the vulnerable women and children is fundamentally built on his lies. Therefore, it does not come as a surprise that his set-up starts crumbling as these lies are discovered, because they are the very seeds of his downfall which he planted with blithe disregard.

It is also important to remember Alexander's parallel psychological process here. Up until Leo's disappearance, Alexander is completely unaware of Gregori's malevolent manipulation. Only after realising that his mother is aware of what is going on but chooses to look the other way, he feels betrayed by both her and Gregori. This rather tragic awakening brings an early emotional maturity. In order to save Tobias from the same fate, he decides to leave the compound with him. By this heroic act he not only separates from Susanna and Gregori (mother and father figure) physically, but also psychologically. When Gregori confronts him condescendingly, Alexander does not hesitate to reach for his gun to end Gregori's rule.

When Tacey (1997) mentions Shakespeare's *Hamlet* (1603), he refers to the eternally repeating pattern of conflict between patriarchs and their sons/successors. In *Hamlet*, King Claudius, who is Prince Hamlet's uncle, kills the prince's father King Hamlet, marries his mother, and usurps the throne. The play focuses on the inner struggle, indecisiveness, and the attempts of Prince

Hamlet to reclaim the throne as the rightful successor. The tragedy of Hamlet appears as him being trapped in a difficult approach-avoidance conflict. If he wants to restore justice and order in the kingdom then he must kill his uncle, reclaim the throne, and rule the land as the new honourable king. But killing Claudius also makes Hamlet a murderer of the king, as cruel and as vile as his uncle. While Tacey notes that killing fathers is not the solution, as it traps the sons in a cycle of violence and misery which echoes in future generations, he acknowledges that this archetypal and intergenerational struggle (which goes all the way back to the Greek myths of Cronus (Kronos) and Zeus, who both overthrew their fathers) is recreated and replayed in contemporary sociopolitical upheaval against hegemonic masculinity which symbolises mercilessness, criminality, and corruption.

In Alexander's case, it is true that the director does not show the actual death of Gregori. However, it is obvious that Alexander knows he will end up like Leo, because he has already started questioning and rejecting Gregori's requests. Therefore, the only way to save his own life and his brother's is to kill Gregori, not only ending a cycle of childhood with violence but also starting a new cycle, a new life with a destructive deed. Erich Neumann (1954) describes this highly metaphorical emancipatory act as a necessary destruction because, as explored in Chapter One in a different context, every child deserves to exist as an individual, not as an extension of their parents' will or as a vessel to fulfil their parents' wishes but as a fully genuine, unforced, and separate being free from the influence of their parental figures. For that reason, death, separation, or neutralising the supremacy of parents becomes a necessary rite of passage for children.

The tragedy in *Partisan* is that the story depicts this metaphorical ending and separation in its most violent and literal form. Especially when Gregori belittles Alexander with his last words, he seals his own fate because he reveals the ugliness he has been hiding all along. Alexander is then left with no choice but to physically manifest this destruction in order to survive, escape this oppression, and begin anew. When he says to Gregori that he wants to do whatever he wants on his twelfth birthday, that wish does not really sound selfish or childish. He truly does want to do something else apart from killing people. He wants to experience life without constantly adhering to Gregori's rules, without following the direction Gregori has set for him, without being the murderous hand, the extension of Gregori. In other words, he wants to be something different to what Gregori wants him to be. He wants to be something more. He wants to be himself without the fear of being killed by this paternal figure.

As mentioned in Chapter 1, this is another aspect of 'father hunger' (Hollis, 1994), the simple need which all children have. This simple need is to be acknowledged, to be affirmed, accepted, and loved as they are by their fathers. If this need is not met, if children realise that they have to behave in certain ways in order to win their fathers' approval, then their individuation process is hampered, or worse, their psyches are wounded by an identity rejection which triggers thoughts and feelings of unworthiness that echo throughout their adult lives.

Individuation, according to Jung, is a lifelong journey. During this journey, people become aware of their own uniqueness, their relation to the collective, their role and place in the bigger story of humanity. In this context, Alexander, at the age of twelve, does not have the adult capacity and knowledge to verbalise these details. However, by making an explicit choice he takes a giant step into his own individuation journey. By leaving his chain and the place he knew as home behind, by protecting innocence and hope symbolised by his baby brother in his arms, he dares to be different than all the rest of the child soldiers. Even though Alexander starts his own journey with violence, Kleiman tends to hint that in this new generation, in this cycle, there is still a chance that things might be different. Will Alexander succeed? Or will he become a part of another cycle of violence? The jury is out.

From manipulating father to abusive father

A father who uses his emotional intelligence to deceive and manipulate everyone around him, including his children, is certainly a proper example of a dangerous man. Of course, this manipulation leads to the abuse of trust established between him and others. This is why Kermode's (2016) description of the film is accurate: *Partisan* is definitely a portrait of stolen innocence. But it is also the portrait of an abused innocence. Kleiman's chilling film shows that seemingly loving, benevolent, and generous protectors can also be cruel, spiteful, dangerous, and have a sinister agenda underneath their charismatic appearance. Daring to say no to them, or to test their authority can simply be deadly.

The next chapter will venture deeper into the troubled bonds between negative fathers and their children. This time abuse will not be covert. It will be visible, physical, sexual, and sometimes financial. The exploration of the darkness in fatherhood will have a distressing look at abusers and how their children suffer because of these men, even many years later when the weight of stolen innocence becomes the burden of a lifetime.

Notes

1   Derived from *sicarius* (meaning 'dagger') in Latin, it is a term used for killer-for-hire. Historically, it goes back to a group of Jews opposing the Roman rule who were hired to kill Romans and their sympathisers with their daggers. *Sicarii* (Daggermen) was also the name of a Jewish terrorist group in Israel which opposed the Israeli-Palestinian peace process during 1989 and 1990.
2   This real-life hit-and-run set-up is fully replicated in the film.
3   This savage existence is also the main focus of Whyman's (2005) novel *Boy Kills Man*.

4 The symbolic chain, namely the fraternal bond of the Freemasons, is another example of this intimacy and support, physically expressed by holding hands in a circle,
   highlighting their brotherhood and collective power/work.
5 An echo of this masculinity worship can be found in ancient Rome. Mars was the god
   of war and agriculture, and the sire of Romulus who was the founder and the first king
   of Rome. His temples were forbidden to the female sex. If women wanted to worship
   Mars in his temple, they had to drop their female attire and put on male clothing
   (Scott, 1966).
6 This song is specifically written by Joseph Mount for the film, and performed by
   Joseph Mount and Robyn, under the pseudonyms Tony Primo and Nixxie. Its
   video, which is also shown in the film, can be found on YouTube. The video features a heterosexual couple trying to run away from a policeman who tries to arrest
   the man. This crime and punishment angle of the video might provide further
   information on Gregori's psyche, but it is beyond the scope of this chapter.
7 DSM-5 refers to psychopathy as a sub-category of Antisocial Personality Disorder
   (ASPD) but does not recognise it as a psychiatric disorder.

References

Filmography

Cria Cuervos. (1976) Directed by C. Saura. Spain.
Partisan. (2015) Directed by A. Kleiman. Australia.

Bibliography

Aeppli, E. (1960) *Der Traum und seine Deutung*. Zurich: E. Rentsch.
Bacon, A. M. and Regan, L. (2016) 'Manipulative relational behaviour and delinquency:
   Sex differences and links with emotional intelligence', *The Journal of Forensic Psy-
   chiatry and Psychology*, 27, 331–348. https://doi.org/10.1080/14789949.2015.1134625.
Berntsen, D. and Rubin, D. C. (2006) 'The centrality of event scale: A measure of
   integrating a trauma into one's identity and its relation to post-traumatic stress
   disorder symptoms', *Behaviour Research and Therapy*, 44(2), 219–231.
Biedermann, H. (1996a) 'Chain', in *The Wordsworth Dictionary of Symbolism*. Ware:
   Wordsworth Editions.
Biedermann, H. (1996b) 'Hen', in *The Wordsworth Dictionary of Symbolism*. Ware:
   Wordsworth Editions.
Charles, M. (2021) 'In Colombia, child soldiers play many roles', available at: https://
   insightcrime.org/investigations/in-colombia-child-soldiers-play-many-roles/.
Chevalier, J. and Gheerbrant, A. (1996a) 'Child', in *The Penguin Dictionary of Sym-
   bols*. London: Penguin.
Chevalier, J. and Gheerbrant, A. (1996b) 'Necklace', in *The Penguin Dictionary of
   Symbols*. London: Penguin.
Connell, R. W. (1987) *Gender and Power: Society, the Person, and Sexual Politics*.
   Sydney: Allen & Unwin.
Connell, R. W. (2000) *The Men and the Boys*. Sydney: Allen & Unwin.
Davis, S. K. and Nichols, R. (2016) 'Does emotional intelligence have a "dark" side?
   A review of the literature', *Frontiers in Psychology*, 7, article 1316.

Delgado, M. (2010) 'Teenage "sicarios": Colombia's child assassins', available at: www.theragblog.com/teenage-sicarios-colombias-child-assassins.

Denov, M. and Marchand, I. (2014) '"One cannot take away the stain": Rejection and stigma among former child soldiers in Colombia', *Peace and Conflict: Journal of Peace Psychology*, 20(3), 227–240. https://doi.org/10.1037/pa c0000039.

Fitzgerald, J. M. (1988) 'Vivid memories and the reminiscence phenomenon: The role of a self narrative', *Human Development*, 31(5), 261–273.

Geis, F. L. (1970) 'The con game', in R. Christie and F. L. Geis (eds) *Studies in Machiavellianism*. New York: Academic Press, pp. 106–129.

Grieve, R. and Mahar, D. (2010) 'The emotional manipulation-psychopathy nexus: Relationships with emotional intelligence, alexithymia and ethical position', *Personality and Individual Differences*, 48(1), 945–950.

Grieve, R., March, E., and Van Doorn (2018) 'Masculinity might be more toxic than we think: The influence of gender roles on trait emotional manipulation', *Personality and Individual Differences*, 138, 157–162.

Hannah, B. (2006) *The Archetypal Symbolism of Animals: Lectures Given at the C.G. Jung Institute Zürich, 1954–1958*. Wilmette: Chiron.

Hollis, J. (1994) *Under Saturn's Shadow: The Wounding and Healing of Men*. Toronto: Inner City Books.

Janoff-Bulman, R. (1992) *Shattered Assumptions: Towards a New Psychology of Trauma*. New York: The Free Press.

Jung, C. G. (1957) *The Collected Works of C. G. Jung, Volume 1: Psychiatric Studies*. Princeton: Princeton University Press.

Jung, C. G. (1973) *The Collected Works of C. G. Jung, Volume 2: Experimental Researches*. Princeton: Princeton University Press.

Jung, C. G. (1961) *The Collected Works of C. G. Jung, Volume 4: Freud & Psychoanalysis*. Princeton: Princeton University Press.

Jung, C. G. (1971) *The Collected Works of C. G. Jung, Volume 6: Psychological Types*. Princeton: Princeton University Press.

Jung, C. G. (1967) *The Collected Works of C. G. Jung, Volume 7: Two Essays on Analytical Psychology*. Princeton: Princeton University Press.

Jung, C. G. (1969) *The Collected Works of C. G. Jung, Volume 9 (Part 1): Archetypes and the Collective Unconscious*. Princeton: Princeton University Press.

Jung, C. G. (1970) *The Collected Works of C. G. Jung, Volume 11: Psychology and Religion: West and East*. Princeton: Princeton University Press.

Kermode, M. (2016) 'Partisan review – unsettling tale of a violent Pied Piper', *The Guardian*, 10 January, available at: www.theguardian.com/film/2016/jan/10/partisa n-ariel-kleiman-child-assassins-film-review.

Kilduff, M., Chiaburu, D. S., and Menges, J. I. (2010) 'Strategic use of emotional intelligence in organizational settings: Exploring the dark side', *Research in Organizational Behavior*, 30, pp.129–152.

Neumann, E. (1954) *The Origins and History of Consciousness*. London: Routledge & Kegan Paul.

Paulhus, D. L. and Williams, K. M. (2002) 'The dark triad of personality: Narcissism, Machiavellianism, and psychopathy', *Journal of Research in Personality*, 36(6), 556–563. https://doi.org/10.1016/S0092-6566(02)00505-00506.

Ramji, R. (2015) 'Partisan', *Journal of Religion & Film*, 19(1), article 12.

Ronnberg, A. and Martin, K. (eds) (2010a) 'Hen/rooster', in *The Book of Symbols: Reflections on Archetypal Images*. Cologne: Taschen.

Ronnberg, A. and Martin, K. (eds) (2010b) 'Cat', in *The Book of Symbols: Reflections on Archetypal Images*. Cologne: Taschen.

Salovey, P. and Mayer, J. D. (1990) 'Emotional intelligence', *Imagination, Cognition and Personality*, 9, 185–211.

Samuels, A., Shorter, B., and Plaut, F. (2005) *A Critical Dictionary of Jungian Analysis*. London: Routledge.

Scott, G. R. (1966) *Phallic Worship: A History of Sex & Sexual Rites*. London: Senate.

Shapiro, E. (2012) 'Straight indiscretions or queer hypocrites: Public negotiations of identity and sexual behaviour', in S. Hines and Y. Taylor (eds) *Sexualities: Past Reflections, Future Directions. Genders and Sexualities in the Social Sciences*. London: Palgrave Macmillan. https://doi.org/10.1057/9781137002785_7.

Tacey, David J. (1997) *Remaking Men: Jung, Spirituality and Social Change*. New York: Routledge.

Variety. (2015) 'Ariel Kleiman on the challenge of creating "Partisan"', available at: www.youtube.com/watch?v=Mh6nzTwiBLA.

Waddell, C., Van Doorn, G., March, E. and Grieve, R. (2020) 'Dominance or deceit: The role of the Dark Triad and hegemonic masculinity in emotional manipulation', *Personality and Individual Differences*, 166, 110160. https://doi.org/10.1016/j.paid. 2020.110160.

Weiner, M. O. and Gallo-Silver, L. P. (2019) *The Complete Father: Essential Concepts and Archetypes*. Jefferson: McFarland & Company.

Whyman, M. (2005) *Boy Kills Man*. London: Hodder Children's Books.

Chapter 3

The abuser

During the Barbra Streisand in Concert tour (*The Concert*, 1994), which started on 31 December 1993 and ran through 1994, the famous American singer, actor, and director Barbra Streisand dedicated a song in her set list specially to her son, Jason. Taken from the Broadway musical *Sweeney Todd: The Demon Barber of Fleet Street*, this famous 1979 Stephen Sondheim song called 'Not While I'm Around' encapsulates the character Tobias Ragg's wish to protect another character, Mrs Lovett, from all the evils of the world as he sees her as a loving mother figure. Streisand, in her concert, slightly changed the contextual relationship and expressed instead her desire to keep Jason safe from harm and injury, like any good parent would want and do in real life.

Unfortunately, not all parents are good. As explored in previous chapters, they can cause harm with their deliberate absence, or their malevolent manipulation when they are present. Ignoring a child can trigger profound attachment issues, and influencing a child's behaviour with dishonest aims is taking advantage of that child's trust. Parents, however, cause even more harm when they try to control their children extensively, and treat them in a cruel, violent way. In other words, they become abusers.

The *Oxford English Dictionary* defines the word abuse in three different ways. Synonymous with 'misuse', abuse can mean the wrong and harmful usage of something, for example alcohol. Rude, offensive, and hurtful remarks are also defined as abuse. The last definition brings a rather tangible and unmistakable quality to the word's definition: abuse is the heinous, undeserved, and most of the time, physically violent treatment of somebody. This cruel treatment causes injury to the body, and it can leave not only visible scars but also deep psychological wounds whether or not it occurs in a sexual context.

Parental abuse is one of the most thorny and taboo subjects for any filmmaker. Whether it is psychological, sexual, or in the form of physical torture, whether it is fiction, biography, or documentary, abuse is depicted on the silver screen and TV in many ways. *La petite Aurore, l'enfant martyre* (1952), *Mommie Dearest* (1981), *Something About Amelia* (1984), *The Cell* (2000), *Precious: Based on the Novel 'Push' by Sapphire* (2009),

DOI: 10.4324/9781003394488-3

Postcard to Daddy (2010), *Run* (2020), and more recently *Girl in the Basement* (2021) deal with the helplessness and the misery of children in the hands of their cruel mothers, fathers, or similar parental figures. In other words, and as a contrast to Sondheim's song, these children are harmed especially when their parents are around.

This chapter will build on the first two and look at abusive fathers. To explore this dark topic, I will examine two films: *Magnolia* (1999); and *This Boy's Life* (1993), the former being fiction, and the latter a true-life story. They depict the horror, despair, and the suffering of children in bleak and sometimes nightmarish ways. However, as these films also highlight the idea of resilience, they offer interesting perspectives and bring hope to the table as well. But first, I will present a brief contextual review of child abuse and some of the academic engagements with this harrowing subject.

Child abuse: definitions, types, and consequences

Both in the UK and USA, the ongoing argument is that, statistically speaking, the acts of child abuse have not multiplied. However, because the general awareness of public as well as institutional knowledge and perception have increased, it has led to better monitoring and effective reporting (National Research Council, 1993; Lyon, 2003) The combined result of this awareness and reporting has added to the constantly growing visibility and the open discussion of child abuse especially through the twentieth and twenty-first centuries.

The United Nations Convention on the Rights of the Child 1989 and European Convention on Human Rights and the Human Rights Act 1998 act as two main international human rights texts that continue to serve as legal sources for country or territory-specific laws regarding the definition, identification, monitoring, prevention, and the punishment of child abuse. Even though the maltreatment of children is a complex problem, historically it was only perceived and identified in the form of a battered and bruised child, indicating physical abuse. With growing research and reporting, the categories of child abuse now also include sexual abuse, neglect, psychological/emotional abuse, and system abuse.

Apart from system abuse, in each category, there is a range of observable behaviours which broadly overlap with Gough's (1987) description of two main features when it comes to defining what child abuse is: that a child is injured or harmed; and that injury or harm was intended by another person. In child physical abuse, it can be bruising or abdominal trauma, head trauma or fractures (with or without using an object) (Lane et al., 2011), cutting or pricking with an object (including female genital mutilation; Walby et al., 2017), burns (including ice burns, or using cold liquids or objects), or factitious disorder imposed on a child by their caregiver (also known as Munchausen syndrome by proxy). Child sexual abuse may refer to unwanted incestuous behaviours, sexual rituals, exposure to pornography or indecent acts, inappropriate touching or fondling of genitals, or forced prostitution (Mathews and Collin-Vézina, 2019). Neglect can refer to parent/carer failures in providing the physical, medical, educational, moral-legal, and emotional needs of a child (Rebbe, 2018; Blumenthal, 2021), or simply abandonment. Psychological/emotional abuse includes confinement/restriction of movement, bullying, name-calling/verbal abuse, belittlement (Shull, 1999), or deliberate (and sometimes frequent) acts to trigger fear or alarm in order to control a child's behaviour or make fun of them. System abuse, on the other hand, can be iatrogenic (meaning, caused by medical examination or treatment which aims to correct/cure but ends up harming a child) (Henckes, 2021) or the result of a political conflict where the aim for common good overrides the rights of individual children (Cairns, 1989). Apart from these distinct categories, childhood exposure to domestic violence, a term for children and adolescents witnessing intimate partner violence (in the form of violent treatment of their mothers or caregivers) is also one of the reported forms of child abuse, for example in Canada (Lefebvre et al., 2013; Fallon et al., 2015). Financial or economic abuse mentioned in the Duluth abuse of children wheel[1] (Duluth Model, 2023), which covers acts such as using money to control a child's behaviour, wasting family money, embezzling money that belongs to a child, or withholding child support, is also another rather under-researched type of child abuse.

Regardless of its category, adverse childhood experiences can lead to physical, behavioural, mental, emotional problems in adulthood which can hinder any and every social interaction. In other words, and as Corby (2000) notes, not only the abused children pay a terrible cost, but their relatives, friends, partners, and society in general are negatively affected as well. Research into the short, medium, and long-term effects of child abuse has also complex problems. There is a lack of consensus when it comes to defining what child abuse is due to cultural differences around the globe. Methodological issues in research, such as sampling, control groups, and case follow-up, make the attempts in establishing the causality problematic. Plus, there is also the issue of children's possible repression or denial of abuse, unwillingness to share or fear of sharing details of their abuse due to a threat of reprisal. This complexity makes not only the detection of but also the research into child abuse very difficult.

Steele (1986) noted that children can and do recover from injuries and they are not necessarily harmed by them. What harms them, he added, is when these injuries are caused by people who these children loved or thought they would protect them. Therefore, echoing Gough's description mentioned earlier, the worst type of harm and trauma is caused when there is conscious intention of a loved one. In other words, the violation of love and trust results in the biggest damage which is carried into adulthood. Documented via several case studies, being on the receiving end of intentional physical and/or psychological abuse and neglect in childhood leads to a myriad of problems both short and long term. These problems include: sense of insecurity; lack of self-esteem; people-pleasing behaviour; inability to form or maintain secure attachments; poor educational performance; poor peer relationships; complex mental health problems such as PTSD; internalised sense of victimhood; aggression; drug and/or alcohol abuse; criminality and violence (Carmen et al., 1984; Calam and Franchi, 1987; Mowbray, 1988; Erickson et al., 1989; Sykes and Symons-Moulton, 1990; Kaplan, 1996; Harold et al., 1997). Bierman (2005) also noted that childhood abuse, especially when committed by fathers, can lead to atheism. While it is important to note that most of the time the abuse children are subjected to comes from their own biological parents, other caretakers such as biological parent's significant other, siblings, grandparents, other relatives, stepparents, foster or adoptive parents, baby-sitters, or other non-related people such as teachers, coaches, tutors, or even neighbours who are involved in child-caring tasks with different types and levels of responsibility can easily be abusers themselves or contribute to the abuse through their deliberate inaction.

The father–child relationships depicted in *Magnolia* appear in this heavy and very difficult context. Even though they are fictional, some of the abusive elements of these relationships reappear and can be observed in *This Boy's Life*, which makes these seemingly separate and disconnected films share a common territory where the boundary between fact and fiction blurs. The next section will explore the imaginary universe of *Magnolia*, followed by the real-life experiences of Tobias Wolff.

'I have lots of love to give but no idea where to put it': stories of lost children

Magnolia explored the power of the past, the lingering hurt, and how children are harmed by their parental figures through 188 minutes of relentless human drama. The film came after Paul Thomas Anderson's second film *Boogie Nights* (1997), which is about the porn industry and the Golden Age of Porn, when actors struggled between the image they portrayed in films and the personality they had in real life.[2] When *Boogie Nights* proved to be a critical and commercial triumph, Anderson was told he could do whatever he wanted in his next film. Taking this blank cheque, the director set out to write and direct one of the most complex and interesting films in Hollywood history. Bringing themes of forgiveness, trauma, drug addiction, abused, molested, or abandoned children, negligent parents, cancer, death, chance, and divine intervention together, *Magnolia* not only exhilarated the critics and viewers with its unwavering focus on how the past can affect the present, but also divided them in their love-or-hate reaction to the content. The reviews were so polarised that it was called the best and the worst film of the year simultaneously.

The film is indeed an unceasingly intense narrative of physical, psychological, and emotional suffering from its beginning to its end. What makes it even more interesting is the fact that some scenes and storylines are not entirely fictitious. The late Jason Robards who played Earl Partridge on his deathbed was literally battling with lung cancer during the shooting.[3] Anderson (2000) also revealed during his interview for the shooting script that he started writing it after his difficult experiences regarding cancer which affected his friends and close family. Moreover, Tom Cruise, who plays Frank, had also an irresponsible and abusive father (Lane, 2011; Fischer, 2022). After learning that his father was about to die, Cruise ended up by his bed following years of no contact. This almost uncanny fusion of reality and fiction transforms the film into a larger-than-life event, verging on a therapeutic experience for the director and actors (and possibly some viewers) rather than just being another Hollywood production.

Featuring an ensemble cast of over twenty characters, it is not possible to cover and sufficiently summarise *Magnolia*'s colossal and multifaceted plot in a paragraph. However, at its core, the film brings ten interrelated main characters all centred around one major character, Earl Partridge, a media mogul and a dying man who happens to be the central father (figure) of the film. Years ago (and this is revealed halfway through the film), Earl left his dying wife Lily and their son Frank (Tom Cruise) who he was a little boy. Frank took care of his mother until she died with the help of a female neighbour. He, however, built up so much rage and resentment towards his father and his traumatic past, he reinvented himself as an unashamedly misogynistic, penis-glorifying relationship guru with a fictitious life story excluding Earl. He is now selling a multiple-step programme called 'Seduce and Destroy' to single men, teaching and encouraging them to turn women into sex-starved slaves.[4] Earl's trophy wife Linda Partridge (Julianne Moore), who is now hysterical and suicidal because of Earl's imminent death, is unable to deal with her anticipatory grief due to her growing love for Earl, something she did not feel in the past. Jimmy Gator (Philip Baker Hall), the second father of the film, is the host of the (quite condescendingly titled) quiz show *What Do Kids Know?* – a TV programme produced by Earl's company. Jimmy is also dying of cancer, cheats on his wife Rose Gator (Melinda Dillon) with his assistant, and he is revealed to have molested his daughter Claudia Wilson Gator (Melora Walters), who is now a self-destructive cocaine addict. Rick Spector (Michael Bowen) is the third father in the film who forces his very intelligent (and most probably neurodivergent) son Stanley Spector (Jeremy Blackman) to win the quiz show's jackpot, even though Stanley is bullied by his teammates and neglected by the show's producers. To add to this complexity, there are the simultaneous storylines of the 'Quiz Kid' Donnie Smith (William H. Macy) who got robbed by his parents right after he won the same TV show years ago, the hospice nurse Phil Parma (Philip Seymour Hoffman) who looks after Earl but gets sucked into Earl's rapidly unravelling family drama, and the kind-hearted police officer Jim Kurring (John C. Reilly), who falls in love with Claudia and tries to save her from her impending doom.

During a fateful day in the San Fernando Valley, the lives of these eleven characters and their past – sometimes with the help and sometimes with the hinderance of seventeen supporting characters and further mini-storylines – collide with each other with increasing complexity until a torrential rain of frogs delivers an abrupt pause to their chaotic and painful existence, altering the course of their lives at the end of the film. Just before this seemingly divine intervention, the director also ups the ante by including a collective singalong scene to Aimee Mann's (1999) 'Wise Up' that appears out of the blue (but connects each character in their own moments of inner realisation) and adds to the unconventionally frank and deeply interconnected narrative which makes up the whole film.

After a thought-provoking prologue on fate, chance, and death (which is unrelated to the film's actual storyline but invites the viewers to ponder on the nature of cause and effect), Anderson introduces the children (and where they are now in their lives) one by one[5] in snippets. Frank[6] appears first on a TV commercial, selling his 'Seduce and Destroy' programme to any hot-blooded male interested in 'taming' women. He argues that the only way to bypass the female analytical mind (and make them desire a man) is to use the correct language at the correct time. In other words, manipulation. Later on in the film, when Frank takes the centre stage during his workshop, Anderson depicts him as the ultimate alpha male who performs kickboxing moves, gyrates his hips, thrusts his pelvis, moans, and groans with pleasure to high-light his virility and machismo in front of a young and rowdy male audience which laps it all up with glee like obedient puppies. This I-am-the-top-man attitude of Frank continues at the beginning of his TV interview, conducted by Gwenovier (April Grace). When Gwenovier starts to gently question his fictional background in detail, his bravado slowly fades until she reveals that she is aware of the fact that he is Earl's son. As his past with his neglectful father comes back to haunt him on camera, the interview gets derailed. Frank refuses to talk at first and goes mute, then physically attacks Gwenovier for bringing the topic up about his mother's unfortunate death and unveiling his wounds and powerlessness. Frank's emotionally taxing day reaches an unex-pected climax after Phil convinces him on the phone to visit Earl. Frank breaks down completely and sobs uncontrollably next to his comatose father, confessing how much he still loves him even though Earl abandoned him and caused so much pain.

The second troubled child of the film is Claudia. Now estranged from her father Jimmy and living on her own, Claudia spends her days picking up random men at cheap bars, taking them home, and having sex with them after getting high on cocaine. Even though she refuses to see her father in person, she does not miss an episode of the quiz show on TV, watching him, crying, and taking more cocaine. The reason for her out-of-control and self-destructive life as an adult is revealed towards the end of the film when Jimmy, after being humiliated by Stanley, confesses to Rose 'how he might have touched their daughter inappropriately' when she was a child. This confession coincides with Jim and Claudia's romantic dinner scene where she feels unable to cope with the fact that there can be a man whom she can trust, a man who can love her without abusing or hurting her and accept her unconditionally with her flaws and troubled past. Being rejected and left at the table on his own suddenly, Jim does not give up and goes back to Claudia's apartment after the deluge and convinces her that there is hope for them as a future couple.

Stanley is introduced straight after Claudia. Just like Donnie Smith, he is the victim of his father's greed and simply a showbiz instrument at the hands of Earl's production company. As one of the most gifted children ever to appear on *What Do Kids Know?*, he lives an impossibly chaotic life, trying to balance school and his shooting schedule. On this particular day, he is paired with two other children in a team against a trio of adults who continuously make sneering comments about him to sabotage his success as he is the only erudite competitor in his team. Even though he desperately and repeatedly asks for permission to use the toilet not only before the broadcast starts[7] but also during commercial breaks, the production crew refuses to let him go which leads to him losing control of his bladder live on TV. He loses his temper and lashes out at the host Jimmy Gator who abruptly ends the show after this unexpected public humiliation. Stanley's well-deserved rebellion extends to his father at the end of film where he demands more love and affection from him only to be met with an indifferent attitude.

Donnie Smith,[8] who won the same quiz show thirty years ago and briefly enjoyed the experience of being a celebrity, is the fourth distressed child of the film. As he was a minor at the time, Donnie's parents embezzled all his money and abandoned him. Also struck by lightning twice, Donnie has lost all the intelligence and capabilities that made him a quiz show winner. Appearing as the possible future version of Stanley, he now works as a TV salesman, and his boss takes advantage of his reduced math skills when it comes to his pay cheque. Donnie not only carries the burden of his parent's betrayal as an adult but is also crushed under the weight of his unexpressed desire for men. He is secretly in love with a muscular bartender who wears dental braces, and he is willing to get some for himself so he can build up the courage to start a conversation with the hunk. On this particular day, he experiences an emotional outburst at the bar and confesses his love for the bartender in front of everyone in a heartbreaking way, telling him how much he will love him and be good to him. Unreciprocated, Donnie rushes to the toilet to vomit, feeling ashamed and worthless. Out of despair, he decides to rob the safe of the shop he works at but gets spotted by Jim. As a kind-hearted policeman, Jim does not press charges but makes Donnie put the money back in the safe. As Donnie cries on Jim's shoulder, telling him how he has so much love to give but he has no idea where to put it, Jim offers to befriend him.

It is important to note that Anderson does not save any of his characters from their painful pasts. Especially when it comes to these children, he deliberately focuses on the results of their parental maltreatment which puts them under pressure, making them frenzied and turbulent, leading up to a tremendous release symbolised by the powerful atmospheric condition which hits the valley. Plus, while Stanley's cruel treatment in the present is shown, Anderson does not include any flashbacks for the abuse these children suffered in the past. The individual reasons for them being as they are and for their suffering, however, are revealed slowly to underline the long-term impact of their individual experiences, and to highlight how their past refuses to cease and continues to affect their present.

Magnolia's particular perspective on abusive fathers and how they make children suffer is also the main focus of this chapter's second film, *This Boy's Life*. Where *Magnolia* focuses on parental abuse but does not depict it in full, *This Boy's Life* goes to the other end of the spectrum and portrays it all. The next section will provide a brief outlook on this film and its suffocating atmosphere which starts with a fleeting sense of freedom and hope but descends into a morbid tale of captivity and futility until its intense and explosive finale.

Entitlement, physical violence, and marital rape: every boy's story?

Based on Tobias Wolff's (1989) well-known and poignant memoir of the same name, Michael Caton-Jones shot *This Boy's Life* (1993) in a way that juxtaposed distress and optimism. Wolff's adolescent years in the 1950s, his relationship with his peppy but fragile mother Caroline Wolff, her boyfriend(s) and later on her second husband Dwight Hansen's increasing abuse, and also Wolff's school and behavioural problems throughout these years are all depicted in the film with an inspiring frankness. Even though it is not as unceasingly intense as *Magnolia* in terms of its depiction of human drama, especially its domestic violence scenes are difficult to watch and can be very distressing (if not triggering) for people who witnessed or were on the receiving end of parental abuse.

According to the liner notes for the DVD edition of the film, the *Los Angeles Times* film critic Kenneth Turan described *This Boy's Life* as 'every boy's story'. While I hope that it is not, Turan's description clearly makes reference to the post-war family life in the states as well as the society's (then) established norms and roles for men and women which still reverberate today. In this context, the film proves to be a good example which supports the famous epigram of Jean-Baptiste Alphonse Karr (1862, p. 278): *plus ça change, plus c'est la même chose.* [9]

This powerful coming-of-age story starts with Tobias (Leonardo DiCaprio) and Caroline (Ellen Barkin) driving from Florida to Utah to start a new life in 1957. Tobias (who prefers to be called Jack due to his fascination with the author Jack London) narrates that their family broke up five years ago, following a period of estrangement between his parents which led to his father taking his brother Gregory with him and leaving them. Apparently, Caroline had a new boyfriend called Roy (Chris Cooper) after the divorce. However, he beat her up, and now she is leaving her problems behind, an act which Tobias describes as his mother's usual behavioural pattern. She specifically heads to Salt Lake City (instead of Moab, the uranium capital of the world at the time) with the hope of finding uranium and getting rich. Her fantasies about a comfortable life are swiftly crushed at the Utah State Assay Office as the officer tells Caroline that she has more courage than common sense because there is no uranium in Salt Lake City.

Caroline and Tobias stay in the city for a while (with Tobias's school issues ongoing) until Roy suddenly turns up, bringing Tobias a Winchester Model 61 rifle as a gift and telling them he has a new job there. He partly tries to seduce and partly forces Caroline into having sex with him that night, which Caroline first refuses out of fear then relents in order to protect herself and Tobias from another possible physical confrontation. Her pattern of problem avoidance comes back in full swing when she realises Roy is actively stalking her at her workplace. She decides to start again somewhere away from Roy and asks Tobias where he wants to go. When they cannot find a bus to Phoenix until next morning, the place Tobias chose, they decide to hop on the earliest bus available to Seattle while Caroline fantasises about getting a Certified Public Accountant licence this time.

Six months later, they are sharing a flat with two other single women, Marian (Kathy Kinney) and Kathy (Tracey Ellis). Tobias has now friends but is still skipping school with them to smoke, to write pornographic dialogues for the *Superman* TV series, or simply to enjoy being a nuisance to random people by damaging their cars for fun. The lives of the mother and son irreversibly change for the next few years when Dwight Hansen (Robert De Niro) appears as the seemingly charming single father (with three children) who sweeps Caroline off her feet with his handsome looks, gentlemanly behaviour, and sweet talk.

After a flirtatious period during which Caroline and Tobias stay at Dwight's house in Concrete, where Caroline not only beats Dwight at a shooting competition but also wins the top prize as the only female contestant, Caroline decides to marry Dwight partly out of despair and partly hoping it would be good for Tobias to have a father figure in his life. These naive hopes are dashed swiftly as Dwight forcibly uses Caroline like an object during their wedding night, telling her that he does not want to see her face during sex and establishing a husband's clear and incontestable dominance over his wife.[10]

The rest of the film dials up the tension between Dwight and Tobias. Reminiscent of the themes in *Magnolia*, Dwight forces Tobias to work, keeps all the money Tobias earns, spends it on anything he fancies, sells Tobias's rifle without consent, and dresses it all up as education and character building. He uses Tobias's fascination with scouting and BSA against him to make Tobias more receptive to, and unquestioning towards his increasingly abusive behaviour, including using sparring as a way to beat him up, make him cry, and then mock his powerlessness.

Dwight's oldest children, Skipper (Zack Ansley) and Norma (Carla Gugino) escape their father's tyranny by going away for their university education. However, Caroline's blatant refusal to be a referee between Tobias and Dwight continues to contribute to the overall depiction of a suffocating and voluntary imprisonment of both the mother and the child. As Tobias crumbles under the physical, verbal, and emotional abuse of Dwight, his personality shifts to the worse and he starts to mimic Dwight's behaviour when he is with his school friends, mocking, abusing, or harming anyone he considers weak and vulnerable. His only lifeline comes from Arthur Gayle (Jonah Blechman), a school misfit due to his camp behaviour, who tells Tobias that he is slowly turning into Dwight, and also helps him to falsify his poor school grades for boarding school applications so that Tobias can get away from the abuse.

The last 10 minutes of the film brings a final and a bloody confrontation between the stepfather and the stepson. Hearing that Tobias is accepted by a private school with a full scholarship, and realising that his abusive grip is slipping away, Dwight first beats Tobias, bites his wounded finger, then tries to strangle him right in front of his youngest daughter Pearl (Eliza Dushku). Caroline rescues her son this time and they both run away immediately without packing. The film brings the story full circle, showing Tobias and Caroline embarking on a new life again, but this time going separate ways as individuals.

Caton-Jones uses the majority of Wolff's memoir and skilfully captures the vulnerability, the fear and helplessness of the mother, which appears as an intergenerational problem and is passed down to her child in the worst possible way. Caroline tries to make it on her own without a safety net or support from her ex-husband, but is ultimately defeated by both her dreamy expectations and the inflexible patriarchal culture. She runs away from a man she fears only to end up with another bully who terrorises her and her son on a daily basis. Tobias not only zigzags between loving and hating his mother as he is chained to her life and boyfriend/husband choices in order to survive, but he also has a deep yearning to have an enduring father figure in his life. That is why he tries his best to please Dwight (and Caroline) by obeying his rules and orders and by tolerating his abusive behaviour (even though he hates it).

As a contrast to *Magnolia* where the abuse took place in the past (with the exception of Stanley), *This Boy's Life* captures the day-to-day abuse Wolff endured and survived. Again, where the fictional characters of *Magnolia* are mostly lost in despair, *This Boy's Life* depicts the fighting spirit of Wolff which ultimately saves not only himself but also his mother from a certain masculine nightmare. Even though the film does not show the later life of Wolff, he continued his education and writing, and became a lecturer at Stanford University. In 1985 he received the PEN/Faulkner award for his novella *The Barracks Thief* (1984), and in 2005 President Barack Obama awarded him the National Medal of Arts. In other words, Wolff transformed his suffering by engaging with the art of creative writing and did not let his childhood ordeals (or the toxic masculinity which Dwight symbolises) define his adulthood.

Although these two films depict different situations in different ways, the way they focus on fathers and children make them share a common ground in representing child abuse, broken bonds, and the aftermath. The next section will explore power relations and Jungian perspectives within the context of these two films.

Children are not their parents' property: leaving abusers behind

Wrong (1988) argued that the parent–child relationship, in relation to how power is distributed, is the most asymmetrical relationship of all. This is partly because children come to this world totally at the mercy of their parents, and children's earliest experience is nothing but submitting to that incredible amount of power without a will of their own. Plus, that power is so comprehensive, intense, and extensive that it not only gives shape, form, and limit to everything a child does but also defines their character and future. Therefore, the ripple effect of this power dynamic gets bigger and more profound as children grow and step into adulthood, internalising this asymmetry and (most of the time) repeating their parents' patterns of behaviour in other social contexts and relationships.

When Pringle (1975) described the basic needs of children, he specifically listed four categories: love and security; new experiences; praise and recognition; and responsibility. When children are neglected or ignored, grow up with an angry or easily irritable parental figure, or worse, when they are directly (and sometimes repeatedly) injured by that figure, those basic needs are not met, and these children grow up with a sense of deprivation which they are unable to verbalise and take action to alleviate it. The long-term follow-up studies of Oates (1986) showed that complex issues of poor self-confidence and poor self-respect, lack of trust in people and relationships, behavioural problems continue in many abused children. They encounter considerable difficulties not only in developing and maintaining mutually satisfactory adult relationships, but these difficulties are also transmitted to their children when they become parents themselves.

Magnolia's four tormented children – Frank, Claudia, Donnie, and Stanley – are not depicted as parents themselves. However, the film successfully captures the crippling effects of the maltreatment they endured (and in the case of Stanley, still enduring). Abandoned by his father and left powerless beside his dying mother, Frank recreates himself as a motivational speaker for a deeply misogynistic men's movement just to feel in control, powerful, and masculine, hiding all the hurt and betrayal from his childhood, but proving (and aggressively exhibiting) his manhood to the world. Sexually molested by her father, Claudia is now an insecure, deeply shy woman who can only numb her memories of exploitation through drug use and who can only feel desired when she offers her body to random men while drugged. Robbed of the prize money of $100,000 by his parents after winning the quiz show in 1968, Donnie is now all alone, unable to give or receive love, and steals money from his boss's safe just to impress a bartender, repeating his parents' dishonest behaviour. Stanley, as a 10-year-old boy, is slowly drowning in his own television success, which is a both a media exploitation (and coupled with Donnie's case, a further indirect abuse by Frank's father via his production company) and a parental exploitation. He struggles to meet his father's expectations of him – which is to win the quiz show and earn money. In other words, he is forced to become successful and prove his 'manhood', just like Frank, in front of and applauded by other people. The director clearly establishes that these children have not experienced love, security, encouragement, or praise with a responsible father, and that is the main reason why they feel wounded, disempowered, angry, on the edge, and lost.

In the case of *This Boy's Life*, the film opens with Frank Sinatra's famous song 'Let's Get Away from it All', and shows Tobias and Caroline on the road to a new life, driving away from an estranged father and ex-husband, and an abusive boyfriend. Yet, through his mother's rather poor choices, Tobias ends up in a worse situation with his stepfather rather than getting away from it all. It is important to note that the film does not depict Tobias as an angel before Dwight appears. As Lamb (1986) pointed out, inadequate fathering can lead to delinquency and antisocial behaviour in children. Lacking a stable and loving father, Tobias is portrayed as delinquent, and he keeps creating problems at every school he attends. Especially in one scene (20:05), he and his two friends release the handbrake of a random car just to have fun and let it roll downhill until it crashes into other vehicles. However, when he is alone, he is depicted as a wanderer and a daydreamer while he watches other men in the neighbourhood with their children. As he writes imaginary dialogues for them, he also fantasises about the return of his father (10:53), giving Tobias a hug and bringing presents. This is why Tobias, with an unyielding desire to have a reliable father figure in his life, tries to make his mother happy by being a conscientious and obedient stepson to Dwight, enduring all the abuse Dwight throws at him. In his particular case, unfortunately, the psychological abuse is coupled with the physical and the financial.

As summarised by Paul and Eckenrode (2015), childhood psychological maltreatment has six subtypes: (a) spurning (which includes hostile rejection and degradation); (b) exploiting or corrupting; (c) terrorising; (d) ignoring or denying emotional responsiveness; (e) isolating; and (f) mental, health, and educational neglect. Research has also shown that childhood psychological maltreatment contributes to feelings of worthlessness, hopelessness, depressive symptoms in adolescence, anxiety, and in some cases self-destructive behaviour.

Caton-Jones depicts the frightening, controlling, and quite sadistic nature of Dwight in many scenes. When Tobias is alone with him in the car, he drives recklessly with a smirk on his face just to show off and frighten the little boy. He regularly makes belittling jokes about Tobias's absent father to undermine the bond Tobias has with him. He refuses to give any money towards his education, symbolised by Tobias wearing regular shoes instead of trainers to his PE classes or any of the school tournaments he attends as a team player (which becomes a further public humiliation for him). He continuously belittles his school performance and keeps saying that Tobias will never be able to leave Concrete, a pernicious and false statement which eats into Tobias's self-esteem and his hopes about a better future throughout the film. He makes him shell horse chestnuts every night, forces him to wear old and wrong-sized scout's uniform to humiliate him (while he buys himself new ones using Tobias's money), and he shouts at him or is extremely critical every time Tobias complains or does something he does not approve of. His physical and psychological abuse reaches its maximum before the final fight scene where he pushes the mustard jar into Tobias's eye, then beats him up for not scraping the bits left in it well enough, blaming him for being an ungrateful, wasteful child.

Of course, what is even more suffocating is the position of the mother in the middle of this abusive environment. When Tobias complains about Dwight and his unjust, offensive, and cruel behaviour, Caroline's answer is unsympathetic. She says she does not wake up every morning singing and happy. In other words, her reluctance to take a stand, her inaction, and her internalisation of her victimhood amplifies Dwight's ruthlessness and creates more opportunities for him to have an oppressive grip on both the mother and the child.

As these two films are Hollywood productions, it is not possible to isolate them from the American culture they depict. This is probably why two objects, which are central and indispensable to the daily life of Americans, keep appearing in many scenes and contribute to both the narrative and the difficulties of these children while dealing with their own perceived powerlessness, feelings of being trapped, and the consequences of their fathers' actions. These objects are automobile and gun, and they are intricately connected to the idea of masculinity, power, and the (ab)use of that power.

Jung (CW 12, para. 153), Chevalier and Gheerbrant (1996a), and Ronnberg and Martin (2010a) note that vehicles appear as the active psychological development of an individual journeying forward in time, symbols of the ego, and they represent the identity/persona. Cars in particular are connected to social status, individuality, independence, confidence, and power. In *Magnolia*, all the children are depicted in a car very briefly. While Stanley is unable to drive a car due to his age and is always a passenger with his father driving next to him, Donnie is portrayed as a careless driver who crashes into a shop. Claudia is only shown in a taxi once as a passenger (high on cocaine) on her return from the seemingly disastrous dinner with Jim, and Frank appears in a car parked outside his father's house only once. Through this car symbolism, Thomas Anderson's narrative makes it clear that Donnie and Claudia are not acting in full capacity as individuals or responsible adults, whereas Frank's and Stanley's journeys are physically linked to their fathers, and they cannot escape their fathers' negative power and influence on their lives no matter what they do.

In *This Boy's Life*, the narrative begins with a car. As Caroline drives away to Utah to change her and Tobias's lives, it not only represents her determination to be an independent woman but also is her only means of escape from an abusive boyfriend. Caroline's car breaks down completely after their arrival in Utah. This affects her sense of independence and contributes to her feelings of giving up and accepting the dominance of Dwight later on. Tobias, on the other hand, is shown to drive Dwight's car without permission even though he is underage. Therefore, in his surreptitious 'drive' to rebel there is defiance against the stepfather oppression/abuse as well as a desire to shape his own life and be an individual.

The second universal symbol, namely gun (and its many forms, including pistol and rifle), actually appears in all the films this book focuses on. From *Ad Astra* (2019) in Chapter 1 to *The Accountant* (2016) in Chapter 5, probably no other object brings masculinity and power together in such an explosive way. As Ronnberg and Martin (2010b) note, gun not only provides a shortcut for gaining an advantage and feeling superior over another person, but it also enables self-protection. Fighting and hunting, two deeds historically and traditionally assigned to and associated with males, makes gun ultimately a masculine weapon due to its forcefully penetrative quality and is globally seductive to any gender. Connecting two legal opposites, law-enforcement and criminality, gun is a complex symbol of aggression, violence, dominance, war, as well as compliance, deterrence, and power to defend freedom and peace which all feed into the intricate passions of the male psyche.

Magnolia and *This Boy's Life* depict this masculinity and power dynamic through their use of the gun narrative. The kind-hearted policeman in *Magnolia*, Jim Kurring, goes through an experience of workplace humiliation as he loses his gun in a botched pursuit, the very object he is given to wield power over the community to keep it safe. However, when he reveals this humiliation to Claudia during the dinner scene and talks about how powerless and stupid this made him feel, Claudia is deeply impressed by his frankness and the way he owns his vulnerability without any attempt to protect his male pride. The film swiftly contrasts this scene with Jimmy Gator's suicide with a pistol. As a father and as a man who cannot even openly admit he had sexually abused his daughter, Jimmy (already publicly humiliated by Stanley live on TV) chooses to kill himself instead of facing a bigger scandal.

This Boy's Life's rifle narrative, on the other hand, includes both the mother and the son. When Roy gives Tobias a Winchester as a present, it appears not only as an attempt to strengthen the bond between an adult male and his girlfriend by impressing her son, but also as a legal, socially accepted, and culturally encouraged transfer of power from a man to a boy. When Caroline uses this rifle during the shooting competition as the only female contestant and beats all the males (including Dwight), this small victory lifts up her spirits as a single mother but upsets Dwight terribly. This is probably one of the reasons why he confiscates the rifle straight after he marries Caroline, to establish his dominance and to be in charge of a powerful object which (both literally and symbolically) can empower his wife and stepson and bring about his downfall very easily.

When it comes to abuse, Jung himself was no stranger to sexual violence or asymmetric relationships. In his letter to Freud, dated 28 October 1907, he disclosed that when he was a boy, he was sexually assaulted by a man he once worshipped (McGuire, 1974, p. 95). In the same letter, he wrote that his respect and admiration for Freud could be likened to a 'religious crush', and he also admitted its erotic undertone. His turbulent and erotic relationship with Sabina Spielrein[11] while he was married (Noll, 1997; Kerr, 1994) firstly as her analyst and later on as her colleague (which is a boundary violation in doctor–patient and co-worker relationships; Loewenberg, 1995) further complicated not only his entanglement with Freud but also contributed to the theoretical disregard of Spielrein by both men. Although Launer (2015) challenged some of the assumptions regarding this affair in his paper years later, Kerr (1994) argued that both Freud and Jung found Spielrein's contribution to psychoanalytic theory easy to ignore as she was never taken seriously as a patient-turned-theorist, and her views were easily eclipsed by them especially during their deeply divisive and entrenched intellectual clash.

Even though the word 'abuse' does not appear in the general index of Jung's *Collected Works*, it can be found in Volumes 1–19 several times. Jung, however, used this word in a severely restricted context, and he almost always referred to either alcohol/substance abuse or verbal abuse without directly focusing on abuse that can occur in parent–child relationships.[12] On the other hand, he comparatively wrote more about the significance of father and the father archetype, examining its historical and cultural associations.

Jung (CW 4, para. 728–729) argued that human beings automatically inherit many things from their ancestors when they are born. Systems, ways of thinking, and types of behaviour are all inherited, some of which have become instinctual over millions of years of human existence on this planet. These congenital traits and behavioural patterns (in other words, universal forms) serve as the basis of Jung's archetypes (primordial images as well as hypothetical entities) which effect both the individual and the collective psychology around the globe. The father archetype, in this context, is undeniably and inevitably connected with the notion of power. Jung (CW 10, paras 65–66) noted that this solar/masculine archetype corresponded to the Chinese *yang* (as opposed to *yin*, the mother archetype which is lunar/feminine), and it determined our relationship and dealings with other people, with the law, state, authority (King), and territories/boundaries (as in Fatherland). Corresponding to the element air, it represented reason and mental activity (Logos), creativity, and therefore connected to the skies, the heavens, the firmament,[13] where God (the Supreme Creator, or simply, Heavenly Father) dwelled and ruled. The father also represented rules, regulations, divine and moral commandments, and prohibitions (CW 5, para. 396), not only creating but also defining man's life and its limits.

If father represents authority and power, then what happens when that power is misused? What happens when the king/warrior turns into a tyrant/sadist? What happens when the father one sees as a hero, as an inspiring leader, or simply as a loving, protective, strong figure at home, uses that power against them, to harm them (and other loved ones) willingly? Singleton (2003) wisely observed that a child's notion of fathering is formed of three different layers: their direct experience with their personal father (or lack of); the father archetype's influence on them; and the internalisation of their mother's interpretation/experience of their father. Therefore, if the direct experience with the father is negative, if the father administers his power in a punitive and merciless way, and if the mother does not/cannot challenge or put a stop to this experience, then that father becomes the abuser who casts a very long shadow over the children throughout their adult lives.

In these two films, the mothers are not depicted positively either: the mother is either absent (as in Stanley's story); powerless to stop or at least unwilling to challenge the father for the child's benefit (as in Frank's and Tobias's stories); cooperating with the father (in Donnie's story); or simply unaware of the abuse (in Claudia's story). This lack of maternal presence (or resistance) either maintains the unhealthy domestic status quo or makes the fathers bolder in their abusive behaviour[14]. It contributes to their transgression of legal and moral responsibilities which instils a sense of powerlessness, loss, and betrayal in their children which make them feel deeply unhappy and broken.

Engel (2023) clearly noted that some abusers are abused by another in the past and this is why they repeat the same behaviour. Meaning, they are trapped in their hurt and shame and become abusers themselves. She, however, also acknowledges that there are also malignant narcissists and sociopaths who do not and will not take any responsibility for their abusive behaviour. This means that any attempt to reason with them or to correct their behaviour is meaningless and futile. As explored in Chapter 2, research suggests that there might be no hope of change for these people. While *This Boy's Life* clearly depicts this hopelessness in the character of Dwight, *Magnolia* portrays a tiny ray of hope through the character of Frank's father, Earl. In his long and sobering soliloquy about regret, Earl confesses his shame and wrongdoing. However, this long-overdue confession comes only a few hours before his death, and it is not heard or acknowledged directly by Frank. Therefore, the father and the son never manage to heal their broken relationship in a meaningful way, or face to face and in real time.

So, is there a solution to the problem of an abusive father who does not feel remorse for his behaviour? Jung (1973), in one of his letters dated 18 August 1936, described parents as trees and children as fruits which fall from these trees when they ripen. Through this metaphor, he makes it clear that children are not property, they do not belong to their parents like an object would. They are only produced by them. He also adds that children should leave their parents as soon as they reach maturity so that they can lead their lives as independent adults. This perspective forms the theoretical standpoint of many post-Jungian analysts. As mentioned in Chapters 1 and 2, separating from the parent is a necessary step in individuation. Therefore, a complete separation from an abusive parent appears as the only solution, not just for the child's individuation process but, above all else, for protecting the physical and psychological well-being of that child whether or not they have reached maturity. This is especially necessary when that parent shows no remorse for the damage they cause and will continue to treat their child as their property.

In *This Boy's Life*, Tobias leaves his abusive stepfather behind and never looks back (except years later in his memoir, but this time as a cautionary and educational story). This complete separation presents itself as the only option because Dwight tries to strangle him in front of Pearl and Caroline. Therefore, it is literally a choice between staying or dying. In *Magnolia*, this separation is less violent. While Claudia is already living away from her father and refuses to see him, Stanley confronts his father non-aggressively. When he tells his dad that he should be nicer to him, he not only invites him to take responsibility for his actions but also makes sure his dad understands that he will not continue to tolerate his abuse (indicating a future separation). For the other two children, Frank and Donnie whose fathers are never coming back to hurt them again, the path to rescuing their inner child (though not shown) definitely includes working with a mental health professional in order for them to cultivate self-compassion and happiness as individuals.

From abusive father to murder in the family

The famous German playwright and poet Bertolt Brecht once said the human race has a distinct tendency to remember the abuses it has been subjected to rather than words and acts of love. This is because, he argued, nothing substantial remains after a kiss, whereas wounds leave scars. *Magnolia* and *This*

Boy's Life depict how some of these scars are life-changing and may never go away completely, especially if they are caused by parental figures who were expected to protect and care for their children.

An abusive father harms a lot of things in a child: personality; ability to trust another human being; mental faculties; creativity; and of course, regard for one's own well-being and happiness. But probably the biggest and the most tragic of all is that he harms the future potential of that child, their capability to dream of a better future. By diminishing the hope that every child is instinctively and innately drawn towards, he cripples his child's future and sentences them to a bleak existence where every success or pleasure is somewhat lacking, less colourful, or incomplete. In other words, he depletes the joy of living.

For children like Frank, Claudia, Stanley, Donnie, and Tobias, the past does not go away, it does not simply cease to be. Even years later, the abuse they endured is still there, embodied. It continues to influence the present in different ways, even when they do not look back. So, is there a way to end this cruelty, this tyranny of the past? Iris Murdoch's (1968) suggestion might be one of the very few options left: deliberately looking at the good, instead of looking at the evil. She suggests that focusing on the good intentionally, in ourselves and in other people, breaks the past's reign of terror on the present. Only in the light of good, she adds, can evil be seen in its place, without being influential or being owned. Just there, only existing.

The next chapter will look at evil, again from a domestic perspective. This time, however, the asymmetrical power relation between a parent and a child will be taken to its limits. Verbal, physical, and sexual abuse will result in murder within the family. The negative father's path now leads to the horrors of filicide and patricide.

Notes

1 Developed in the 1980s by Ellen Pence and Michael Paymar (Pence and Paymar, 1993), the original Duluth Model had the focus on male violence against women, listing different types of power and control. Over the years, this model has preserved its fundamentals and also become a useful template identifying other acts and shades of coercion, threat, neglect, violence and abuse which are present in other contexts such as culture, religion, immigrant and minorities, LGBT+, and animals.
2 This typical 'persona' theme that runs through the porn industry (both yesterday and today) is also an under researched topic in Jungian studies.
3 Another interesting connection with Jason Robards is that he also played a patriarch called Frank Buckman in the film *Parenthood* (1989). In this film, he wants to have a son who can 'piss with the big guys' and his parenthood desires have unintended consequences as his favourite child Larry (Tom Hulce) becomes a compulsive gambler and a negligent parent as he tries to live out his father's ambitions.
4 The programme is so over the top, one cannot help but gasp in disbelief at the names of some of its training modules and taglines. Inviting participants to respect penis power instead of vagina, or to pretend that they are kind and compassionate

just to seduce women, reveals not only the aggressive, manipulative, and hegemonic masculine attitudes, but can also be considered as the herald of social media
influencers such as Andrew Tate who was, at the time of writing, detained
in Romania for alleged sexual assault and exploitation (Weaver, 2023). In a
nutshell, the Seduce and Destroy programme appears as art imitating life in a
perfect manner.

5 These character introductions are presented with the song 'One', covered by Aimee
Mann playing in the background. Originally from Harry Nilsson's 1968 album
Ariel Ballet, and famous for its line declaring one as the loneliest number, it sug-
gests that the characters (especially the children) are feeling lonely and lost.

6 Anderson (2000) based Frank T. J. Mackey's character on Ross Jeffries, a seduc-
tion and pick-up artist who uses NLP-based techniques to seduce women.

7 Anderson (2000) reveals that this toilet ban was actually a real-life experience of
Fiona Apple, his then girlfriend. The way her managers did not let her use
the bathroom and forced her to perform on stage got incorporated into Stanley's
storyline.

8 Again, Anderson (2000) notes that this character is based on unlucky child celeb-
rities like Gary Coleman and Jackie Coogan, who were embroiled in legal battles
with their parents regarding the money they earned through TV shows and Hollywood films.

9 Meaning 'the more things change, the more they stay the same', this aphorism
looks at human nature and the concept of change in a rather pessimistic way. It
underlines the perspective that things, events, and people's actions might bring
change over the course of time, but the core of human nature and the status quo it
reinforces does not and will not change.

10 The United States legal system did not recognise or criminalise marital rape on all
Federal lands until the Federal Sexual Abuse Act in 1986 (Bennice and Resick,
2003) due to the established cultural norms and rules which did not allow a wife to
deny her husband sex. It was considered that, through the matrimonial contract,
she had given her full consent to intercourse which was not retractable.

11 This affair and its aftermath, including the way it affected Freud, Jung, and
Spielrein, was the main focus of David Cronenberg's film *A Dangerous Method*
(2011), which was also based on Kerr's (1994) book.

12 A similar situation can be observed for the word 'assault'. For example, Jung wrote
about assault in relation to erotic dream imagery of women (CW 5, para. 8) or
examined sexual assault in Ojibwe mythology (CW 5, para. 487). But then again,
this focus does not translate into a specific section on sexually violent parents and
the effect of this violence on children.

13 The idea of the firmament appears to have a special connection with *Magnolia*.
During his interview, Anderson (2000, p. 198) reveals that the film's title comes
from the notion of 'magonia', and he describes it as the mythical place above the
firmament which stores everything awful and unhealthy on Earth. When this
place reaches its capacity and cannot contain anything anymore, it then opens up
and pours everything back down to Earth. This mythical (and spiritual) connection with the sky is represented in the film through weather forecasts which
appear several times and warn of heavy rain, suggesting that the meteorological
conditions are building up to a big release. In his truly climactic finale, Anderson
delivers a tempestuous downpour of frogs (which he uses as a biblical reference to
Exodus 8:2, a warning to Pharaoh to release the slaves). Because each child is
wounded by paternal abuse that defines their current predicament and restricts
them, this bizarre weather phenomenon comes across as an unexpected wake-up
call to set themselves free from the awful captivity of their experiences.

14 Tacey (1997) presents a similar perspective in a sociopolitical context. He argues that the patriarchal institutions are not really invested in changing or evolving for the better, and the women who work for these institutions mainly contribute to the replication of patriarchy rather than resisting, challenging, or reforming it.

References

Discography

Mann, A. (1999) *Magnolia: Music from the Motion Picture.* Reprise Records.
Nilsson, H. (1968) *Ariel Ballet.* RCA Victor.
Streisand, B. (1994) *The Concert.* Columbia.

Filmography

A Dangerous Method. (2011) Directed by D. Cronenberg. Canada, Germany, UK.
The Accountant. (2016) Directed by G. O'Connor. USA.
Ad Astra. (2019) Directed by J. Gray. USA.
Boogie Nights. (1997) Directed by P. T. Anderson. USA.
The Cell. (2000) Directed by Tarsem. USA.
Girl in the Basement. (2021) Directed by E. Röhm. USA.
La petite Aurore, l'enfant martyre. (1952) Directed by J-Y. Bigras. Canada.
Magnolia. (1999) Directed by P. T. Anderson. USA.
Mommie Dearest. (1981) Directed by F. Perry. USA.
Parenthood. (1989) Directed by R. Howard. USA.
Precious: Based on the Novel 'Push' by Sapphire. (2009) Directed by L. Daniels. USA.
Postcard to Daddy. (2010) Directed by M. Stock. Germany.
Run. (2020) Directed by A. Chaganty. USA.
Something about Amelia. (1984) Directed by R. Haines. USA.
This Boy's Life. (1993) Directed by M. Caton-Jones. USA.

Bibliography

Anderson, P. T. (2000) *Magnolia: The Shooting Script.* New York: New Market Press.
Bennice, J. A. and Resick, P. A. (2003) 'Marital rape: History, research, and practice', *Trauma, Violence, & Abuse,* 4(3), 228–246.
Bierman, A. (2005) 'The effects of childhood maltreatment on adult religiosity and spirituality: Rejecting God the Father because of abusive fathers?', *Journal for the Scientific Study of Religion,* 44, 349–359. https://doi.org/10.1111/j.1468-5906.2005.00290.x.
Blumenthal, A. (2021) 'Neglect as Collective Failure to Provide for Children: Toward a New Theoretical Approach', *Child Welfare,* 99(3), 31–60.
Cairns, E. (1989) 'Society as child abuser: Northern Ireland', in W. S. Rogers, D. Hevey, and E. Ash (eds) *Child Abuse and Neglect: Facing the Challenge.* London: B. T. Batsford.
Calam, R. and Franchi, C. (1987) *Child Abuse and its Consequences.* Cambridge: Cambridge University Press.

Carmen, E., Rieker, P., and Mills, T. (1984) 'Victims of violence and psychiatric illness', *American Journal of Psychiatry*, 141, 378–383.

Chevalier, J. and Gheerbrant, A. (1996a) 'Vehicle', in *The Penguin Dictionary of Symbols*. London: Penguin.

Corby, B. (2000) *Child Abuse: Towards a Knowledge Base*. Buckingham: Open University Press.

Duluth Model. (2023) 'Wheel library', available at: www.theduluthmodel.org/wheel-ga llery/.

Engel, B. (2023) *The Emotionally Abusive Relationship: How to Stop Being Abused and How to Stop Abusing*. 2nd ed. San Francisco: Jossey-Bass.

Erickson, M., Egeland, B., and Pianta, R. (1989) 'Effects of maltreatment on the development of young children', in D. Cicchetti and V. Carlson (eds) *Child Maltreatment: Theory and Research on the Causes and Consequences of Child Abuse and Neglect*. Cambridge: Cambridge University Press.

Fallon, B., Van Wert, M., Trocmé, N., MacLaurin, B., Sinha, V., Lefebvre, R., Goel, S., et al. (2015) *Ontario Incidence Study of Reported Child Abuse and Neglect 2013: Major Findings*. Toronto, ON: Child Welfare Research Portal. Available at: http://cwrp.ca/sites/default/files/publications/en/ois-2013_final.pdf.

Fischer, W. (2022) 'The tragic real-life story of Tom Cruise', *Grunge*, 25 May, available at: www.grunge.com/875331/the-tragic-real-life-story-of-tom-cruise/.

Gough, D. (1987) 'The Phenomena of Child Abuse'. Report to Scottish Office.

Harold, G. T., Fincham, F. D., Osborne, L. N., and Conger R. D. (1997) 'Mom and Dad are at it again: Adolescent perceptions of marital conflict and adolescent psychological distress', *Developmental Psychology*, 33(2), 333–350.

Henckes, N. (2021) 'Negotiating the limits of therapy – Die Grenzen der Therapie verhandeln: Patients', families' and nurses' perspectives on therapeutic failure in the aftermath of the psychiatric revolution, 1970s–1980s', *Medizinhistorisches Journal*, 56(1/2), 79–102.

Jung, C. G. (1961) *The Collected Works of C. G. Jung, Volume 4: Freud & Psychoanalysis*. Princeton: Princeton University Press.

Jung, C. G. (1967) *The Collected Works of C. G. Jung, Volume 5: Symbols of Transformation*. Princeton: Princeton University Press.

Jung, C. G. (1970) *The Collected Works of C. G. Jung, Volume 10: Civilization in Transition*. Princeton: Princeton University Press.

Jung, C. G. (1973) *Letters of C. G. Jung: Volume I, 1906–1950*. London: Routledge & Kegan Paul.

Kaplan, T. (1996) 'Psychological responses to interpersonal violence: Children', in D. Black, M. Newman, J. Harris-Hendricks, and G. Mezey (eds) *Psychological Trauma: A Developmental Approach*. London: Gaskell, pp. 184–188.

Karr, J-B. A. (1862) *Les Guêpes*. Paris: Michel Lévy Frères.

Kerr, J. (1994) *A Most Dangerous Method: The Story of Jung, Freud, and Sabina Spielrein*. London: Sinclair-Stevenson.

Lamb, Michael E. (1986) 'The changing role of fathers', in M. E. Lamb (ed.) *The Father's Role: Applied Perspectives*. New York: John Wiley.

Lane, C. (2011) *Magnolia*. Chichester: Wiley-Blackwell.

Lane, W., Bair-Merritt, M. H., and Dubowitz, H. (2011) 'Child abuse and neglect', *Scandinavian Journal of Surgery*, 100(4), 264–272.

Launer, J. (2015) 'Carl Jung's relationship with Sabina Spielrein: a reassessment', *International Journal of Jungian Studies*, 7(3), 179–193, https://doi.org/10.1080/19409052.2015.1050597.

Lefebvre, R., Van Wert, M., Black, T., Fallon, B., and Trocmé, N. (2013) 'A profile of exposure to intimate partner violence investigations in the Canadian child welfare system: An examination using the 2008 Canadian Incidence Study of Reported Child Abuse and Neglect (CIS-2008)', *International Journal of Child & Adolescent Resilience*, 1(1), 142–181.

Loewenberg, P. (1995) *Fantasy and Reality in History*. New York: Oxford University Press.

Lyon, C. (2003) *Child Abuse*. 3rd ed. Bristol: Family Law.

Mathews, B. and Collin-Vézina, D. (2019) 'Child sexual abuse: Toward a conceptual model and definition', *Trauma, Violence & Abuse*, 20(2), 131–148.

McGuire, W. (1974) *The Freud/Jung Letters: The Correspondence between Sigmund Freud and C.G. Jung*. London: Hogarth Press/Routledge & Kegan Paul.

Mowbray, C. T. (1988) 'Post-traumatic therapy for children who are victims of violence', in F. M. Ochberg (ed.) *Post-Traumatic Therapy and Victims of Violence*. New York: Brunner/Mazel, pp. 196–212.

Murdoch, I. (1968) *The Nice and The Good*. London: Chatto & Windus.

National Research Council. (1993) *Understanding Child Abuse and Neglect*. Washington, DC: National Academy Press.

Noll, R. (1997) *The Aryan Christ: The Secret Life of Carl Jung*. London: Macmillan.

Oates, R. K. (1986). *Child Abuse and Neglect: What Happens Eventually?* New York: Brunner/Mazel.

Paul, E. and Eckenrode, J. (2015) 'Childhood psychological maltreatment subtypes and adolescent depressive symptoms', *Child Abuse & Neglect*, 47, 38–47. https://doi.org/10.1016/j.chiabu.2015.05.018.

Pence, E. and Paymar, M. (1993) *Education Groups for Men Who Batter: The Duluth Model*. New York: Springer Publishing Company.

Pringle, M. K. (1975). *The Needs of Children*. London: Hutchinson.

Rebbe, R. (2018) 'What is neglect? State legal definitions in the United States', *Child Maltreatment*, 23(3), 303–315. https://doi.org/10.1177/1077559518767337.

Ronnberg, A. and Martin, K. (eds) (2010a) 'Car', in *The Book of Symbols: Reflections on Archetypal Images*. Cologne: Taschen.

Ronnberg, A. and Martin, K. (eds) (2010b) 'Gun', in *The Book of Symbols: Reflections on Archetypal Images*. Cologne: Taschen.

Shull, J. R. (1999) 'Emotional and psychological child abuse: Notes on discourse, history, and change', *Stanford Law Review*, 51(6), 1665–1701. https://doi.org/10.2307/1229533.

Singleton, W. S. (2003) 'The Father Archetype and the Myth of the Fatherless Son'. PhD thesis, Pacifica Graduate Institute.

Steele, B. (1986) 'Notes on the lasting effects of early child abuse throughout the life cycle', *Child Abuse and Neglect*, 10, 283–291.

Sykes, D. and Symons-Moulton, B. (1990) *A Handbook for the Prevention of Family Violence*. Hamilton: Seldom Printing.

Tacey, David J. (1997) *Remaking Men: Jung, Spirituality and Social Change*. New York: Routledge.

Walby, S., Towers, J., Balderston, S., Corradi, C., Francis, B., Heiskanen, M., Helweg-Larsen, K., Mergaert, L., Olive, P., Palmer, E., Stöckl, H., and Strid, S. (2017)

'Different forms of violence', in *The Concept and Measurement of Violence*. Bristol: Policy Press, pp. 57–102.

Weaver, M. (2023) 'Romanian court extends Andrew Tate detention by 30 days', *The Guardian*, 21 February, available at: www.theguardian.com/news/2023/feb/21/andrew-tate-to-be-held-in-romania-for-30-more-days-as-court-extends-detention.

Wolff, T. (1984) *The Barracks Thief*. New York: Ecco Press.

Wolff, T. (1989) *This Boy's Life: A Memoir*. New York: Grove Press.

Wrong, D. (1988) *Power: Its Forms, Bases and Uses*. Chicago: Chicago University Press.

Chapter 4

The murderer

When people say history is written in blood, they usually refer to the deadly struggles of mankind and the victors who lived to tell the tale in the way they wanted. They do not necessarily mean or refer to parricides and bloodbaths that occur in families. Yet, history continues to showcase fathers, mothers, and children turning against each other for different reasons and with different motivations, sometimes for power and sometimes for vengeance. And sometimes what starts as a family affair does not remain within the family. That conflict can be so big, so deep, it can pull other people in and create a bigger chain of destruction.

The bloodshed between family members is an interesting and difficult subject in myths and religions around the globe, and this subject frequently appears in different forms. For example, Teshub the weather god in Mesopotamian mythology, kills his father Kumarbi, the former king of the gods. In Norse mythology, the sorcerer Hreiðmarr gets killed by his sons Fafnir and Regin. The Mahābhārata also tells how a Pandava prince, Babruvahana, kills his father Arjuna during a battle, not knowing Arjuna was his father. In the Western world, Greek myths provide many famous examples. Kronos, the Titan harvest god, castrated (and in some texts killed) his father Uranus, the sky god. Following this event, Zeus, Kronos's son, put an end to his father's rule.[1] In the mortal world, Oedipus, the tragic king of Thebes, killed his father unknowingly and married his mother to become king. Moreover, when Agamemnon, the king of Mycenae, killed his daughter Iphigenia during the Trojan war to appease the goddess Artemis, he attracted the wrath of his wife Clytemnestra who killed Agamemnon with the help of her lover Aegisthus, Agamemnon's cousin. Agamemnon's death was later avenged by his son Orestes who killed his mother Clytemnestra, and only after an intervention by Athena, the goddess of wisdom, came the end of this family carnage. The story of Cain and Abel, a shared narrative in the Tanakh, the Holy Bible, and the Qur'an, also maintains its cultural significance as the first murder committed on Earth according to these religious texts.

As explored in Chapter 3, domestic violence severely harms children, and it does not matter if these children just witness this violence or if they are also

DOI: 10.4324/9781003394488-4

subjected to it. Domestic homicide, on the other hand, is the ultimate form of domestic violence and has many types: intimate partner homicide; parricide (murder of parents); siblicide (murder of siblings); filicide (murder of children) (Mouzos and Rushforth, 2003); neonaticide (murder of a child within the first 24 hours of their life) (Resnick, 1969); familicide (where several family members are murdered by a family member) (Liem et al., 2013); honour/dowry related killings (where a relative, usually a girl/woman, is killed by their family or in-laws due to family reputation sensitivities or conflicts due to a transfer of parental wealth via marriage of a bride) (World Health Organization, 2012); and other family homicides that include cousins, in-laws, and other kin (Australian Institute of Health and Welfare, 2019).

In Chapters 2 and 3, I have looked at two father figures and two children coming very close to murder. Even though Kleiman suggested the impending murder with his tense finale, he did not depict it. Caton-Jones, on the other hand, depicted an attempt by the stepfather who was stopped by the mother. Continuing to portray destructive resolutions to conflicts between family members, this chapter will take a step further and analyse domestic homicide through four films: *The Shining* (1980); *Doctor Sleep* (2019); *Män som hatar kvinnor* (2009) (English title: *The Girl with the Dragon Tattoo*); and *Flickan som lekte med elden* (2009) (English title: *The Girl Who Played with Fire*). Through these films I will explore how and why fathers and their children end up destroying each other. Following the pattern in previous chapters, the analysis will first look at the storylines, themes, and symbols in these films, followed by research on murder, and finally review the subject matter from a Jungian perspective.

Family nightmares in sequels: the masculinity that cuts, burns, and kills

Patricide and filicide, mirroring their prevalence in myths, folklore, and religious texts, is another popular topic in film. From horror and fantasy titles such as *The Omen* (1976), *The Ring* (2002), *Case 39* (2009), and *Guardians of the Galaxy Vol. 2* (2017) to dramedy and satire like *Joe* (1970), from historical drama like *Titus* (1999) to heart-breaking examples such as *Murdered by My Father* (2016), domestic homicide is frequently revisited by several scriptwriters and directors. This topic's rather morbid charms become even more difficult to resist when a film is based on a successful book. Stephen King's third published novel in 1977, *The Shining* (King, 1977), became his second bestseller after *Carrie* (King, 1974). Dealing with supernatural forces and family drama at a haunted hotel called The Overlook, the book was adapted to the big screen by Stanley Kubrick in 1980 with the same name. The same forces (plus others) returned when visitors of King's website voted in favour of *Doctor Sleep* as King's next novel in 2009. When published in 2013 as a sequel to *The Shining, Doctor Sleep* (King, 2013) became an instant hit and prompted another cinematic adaptation, this time directed by Mike Flanagan and released in 2019.

The Shining tells the story of an alcoholic father, ex-teacher, and writer named Jack Torrence (Jack Nicholson), his wife Wendy (Shelly Duvall), and their son Danny (Danny Lloyd), who has telepathic abilities (called 'shining'). The film begins with Jack taking the position as a winter caretaker at the Overlook Hotel in Colorado, where he plans to finish writing his play in peace as the hotel is closed for winter. When they arrive, the leaving manager gives Jack the keys to the hotel and reveals that the last caretaker lost his sanity, killed his family and then himself. As the family settles in, the hotel's head chef Dick Hallorann (Scatman Crothers), who has the same abilities as Danny, warns him that the hotel has an evil 'shine' due to the terrible past events and he should avoid Room 237 for his own protection. Following Dick's departure to Florida, Danny and Jack start to get affected by the hotel's unseen forces in different ways. Jack's mental health starts deteriorating as he loses his temper frequently, is unable to write, and has dreams of killing his family. Danny is lured into Room 237, and Wendy finds him bruised and traumatised, immediately thinking it might be Jack who did it. As Jack starts drinking (sinisterly encouraged by the ghost bartender Lloyd, played by Joe Turker) he falls into a psychotic episode similar to the last caretaker, and chases after Wendy and Danny with an axe. Briefly interrupted by Dick who returns to the hotel after telepathically receiving Danny's call for help, Jack swiftly kills the chef and chases after Danny with a berserk rage through a snow-covered hedge maze. As Danny manages to mislead his father in the maze and reunites with his mother, Jack cannot find them and freezes to death. Wendy and Danny escape using Dick's snowcat, trying to leave the horrors behind.

Doctor Sleep takes the story of Danny (now going by Dan) further into his adulthood. It is revealed that even though he moved to Florida with his mother, and they tried to avoid any memory of their traumatic experience at the hotel (including snow), the spirits from the Overlook did not stop tormenting Dan Torrence (Ewan McGregor) throughout his childhood. Dick Hallorann's spirit (Carl Lumbly) trained Dan to capture those spirits in mental lockboxes, but this did not stop Dan from becoming an alcoholic (like his father was) in order to suppress his 'shining'. After several years of wandering across the United States, he ends up in a small town in New Hampshire, attends Alcoholics Anonymous meetings to stay sober, and works as a hospice attendant to comfort dying people with his abilities (hence the nickname Doctor Sleep). Now in 2019, he is telepathically warned by a teenage girl named Abra Stone (Kyliegh Curran) about a nomadic cult, the True Knot, which kidnaps psychically gifted children and kills them violently to absorb their life force (called 'steam'). As Abra telepathically witnesses the brutal murder of Bradley Trevor (Jacob Tremblay) and contacts Dan, the cult's leader Rose the Hat (Rebecca Ferguson) becomes aware of Abra's power and send all the cult's members to capture her. Dan, with the help of his friend Billy (Cliff Curtis) and Abra's father Dave (Zackary Momoh) manages to kill all the members except Rose, but Dave dies. Dan and Abra decide to lure Rose to the Overlook Hotel so that the evil spirits can capture her. Dan confronts his father's spirit at the hotel who appears as The Bartender (Henry Thomas) and tries to make Dan drink. Dan refuses and fights Rose as a sober man. He unlocks his mental lockboxes to release all the spirits that troubled his childhood, and they devour Rose only to turn on Dan afterwards. Dan warns Abra to leave the Overlook, and he blows up the boiler, burning down the hotel completely to destroy its evil presence. Later on, his spirit, now in peace, appears to Abra and encourages her not to hide her abilities from the world like he did.

The Shining did not get much praise when it was released. It became the only Kubrick film that was nominated for two Razzie awards: the worst director, and the worst actor (for Shelley Duvall). Especially, the way Kubrick changed some elements of the original novel was openly criticised by Stephen King, noting that Kubrick's focus was mainly on the innate evil of human beings rather than an external force taking control of them. While the novel depicts Jack gradually going insane due to the supernatural evil in the hotel, Kubrick's depiction makes it ambiguous – it is entirely possible to argue that the source of horrors is actually Jack's own mind. Also in the novel, Jack regains his sanity, albeit briefly, to help his wife and son escape, and the hotel is destroyed. In the film, however, the hotel stays intact, and Jack's simmering frustration as a man/father/author seems to explode into a murderous rage mainly fuelled by alcohol addiction. The novel makes it clear that the hotel's aim is to capture Danny as he is telepathically gifted but turns to his father instead when unsuccessful. Jack's troubled past is not mentioned in the film, and his main weapon, a mallet, is changed to an axe. Kubrick also added new details to the original story, such as the torrent of blood scene and the Grady sisters scene, which become truly iconic horror segments in cinema history.

The criticism for the film has turned more positive over the years, and especially the arrival of *Doctor Sleep*'s cinema adaptation has contributed to it. Even though this second novel is a direct sequel to the first one, Flanagan managed to write a creative script which not only incorporated items from both the novel and Kubrick's version, but also became an independent sequel to both versions of *The Shining* at the same time in terms of its narrative scope. King is reported to be so impressed with Flanagan's script (Collis, 2019) that he said everything he disagreed with in Kubrick's version was rectified. Flanagan's delicate focus on the damaging impact of alcoholism on human psychology and, in Jack and Danny's case, how it can destroy a father–son relationship was also praised by many.

While *The Shining* and *Doctor Sleep* deal with the destructive and murderous father within a supernatural context, *Män som hatar kvinnor* and *Flickan som lekte med elden* flip the script on this father formula and depict how a child is driven to patricide. Similar to the first two films, they are cinematic adaptations based on the international bestselling crime novel series called the *Millennium* trilogy by the late Swedish author, journalist, and activist Stieg Larsson. Published posthumously, *Män som hatar kvinnor* (Larsson, 2005), *Flickan som lekte med elden* (Larsson, 2006), and *Luftslottet som sprängdes* (Larsson, 2007) focus on how a social misfit and a terrific computer hacker named Lisbeth Salander is pulled into an investigation of murder and a sex-trafficking network of underage girls. The trilogy, which brings high-ranking Swedish individuals and a Soviet defector together in a web of crime, tells the story of Lisbeth not only fighting for her survival but also for legal freedom.

The first film's (and the book's) name, *Män som hatar kvinnor*, literally translates as 'men who hate women', and this theme of misogyny runs through the whole trilogy repeatedly either in male characters' individual actions or the order and organisations they represent. Directed by Niels Arden Oplev, the film starts with the journalist Mikael Blomkvist (Michael Nyqvist) being sentenced to three months in prison due to a libel case brought by a billionaire Hans-Erik Wennerström (Stefan Sauk). While Blomkvist is waiting to go to prison, he is hired to investigate privately the strange disappearance of Henrik Vanger's (Sven-Bertil Taube) niece Harriet Vanger (Ewa Fröling), now presumed dead after so many years. Meanwhile, Lisbeth Salander's (Naomi Rapace) legal guardian is replaced by the state after his heart attack. The newly appointed attorney Nils Bjurman (Peter Andersson) rapes Lisbeth and takes control of her finances. She proves her resourcefulness: first by secretly recording him raping her; and then doing the same thing to him to stop his abuse – she rapes him with a dildo and threatens to go to the police with evidence if he does not comply with her wishes. Lisbeth gets interested in Blomkvist's new assignment as she thinks he is an uncorrupted journalist. When Blomkvist realises his computer is hacked by Lisbeth, he asks her to help him solve the case. As Lisbeth and Blomkvist find out disturbing information about the Vanger family, Lisbeth saves Blomkvist from dying at the hands of Martin Vanger (Peter Haber), the CEO of Vanger Corporation who is not only a Nazi sympathiser but also has been systematically abusing and killing Jewish women, trained by his father. Martin tries to escape but he has a traffic accident. Lisbeth lets him burn to death in his car. The duo discover at the end of the film that Harriet is alive in Australia. Harriet comes back to Sweden and reunites with Henrik. She reveals that she ran away from her father (whom she killed) and her sadistic brother Martin, because they both raped her regularly. As Lisbeth decides to help Blomkvist while he is in jail, she hacks into Wennerström's files and not only exonerates Blomkvist but also discovers a sex-trafficking network.

The sequel, *Flickan som lekte med elden*, follows the events of the first film and continues the storyline of Lisbeth's traumatic past. This time, Lisbeth and Blomkvist are sucked into a bigger web of crime. When Blomqvist's journalist colleague and his girlfriend, who were researching into human trafficking and prostitution in Sweden, are murdered alongside Nils Bjurman, the fingerprints on the gun makes Lisbeth the main suspect. As they both try to solve the mystery individually, it becomes a race against time and the police who think Lisbeth is not innocent based on the evidence. Lisbeth finally cracks the case on her own but gets subdued by her half-brother whom she did not know she had. She wakes up in front of her disfigured father Alexander Zalachenko (Giorgi Staykov), the man she tried to burn alive when she was a child to protect her mother. Zalachenko tells Lisbeth that her mother was simply a 'whore', and despises Bjurman for raping Lisbeth, saying he apparently had no taste in women. In order to save his sex-slave business and to avenge his burns, Zalachenko shoots Lisbeth and buries her alive. Parallel to these events, Blomkvist gathers all the information on Zalachenko and realises that the reason Lisbeth was institutionalised and given a legal guardian was that the Swedish state did not want to reveal a sex trafficker's existence (who happened to be a Soviet defector) in the country by acknowledging his crimes. After Lisbeth digs her way out, she wounds her father with an axe, and stops her half-brother from killing her. Blomkvist turns up right before she loses her consciousness. Lisbeth's half-brother gets arrested while she is airlifted to hospital.

These four films depict fathers who deliberately hurt, abuse, and attempt to kill, but never show any remorse for their actions. In Dan's case, his dark and tragic conversation with his father's ghost in *Doctor Sleep* reveals Jack Torrence had always seen his son as a burden, and never really loved him. Things are not any different in Lisbeth's case either. Zalachencko's hatred for his daughter (not to mention women in general) is still potent and paves the way for filicide in *Flickan som lekte med elden*. Plus, in *Män som hatar kvinnor*, Harriet's suffering at the hands of her father leads to a final conflict where she drowns him in order to stop his sexual abuse. In other words, these characters are forged in trauma caused by unrepentant fathers whose acts are sadistic and who are lost in delusions of grandeur.

In these films, two specific symbols keep reappearing in relation to their heavy storylines: axe; and fire. Connecting the themes of filicide and patricide in a gender-blind way, *The Shining* depicts Jack as the bloodthirsty father running after his wife and son, wielding a big axe with maniacal enjoyment. A similar axe reappears in *Flickan som lekte med elden*, this time in the hands of Lisbeth, incapacitating her father who tried to murder her twice. Normally a tool of iron with a steel edge and a wooden handle, axe is generally used for chopping wood. Its cutting, dividing, and separating power, however, becomes a psychological nadir when it is used as a weapon between blood relatives who truly loathe each other.

As Chevalier and Gheerbrant (1996a) point out, axes generally come crashing down with force. Its speed and penetrating power is connected to thunder, lightning, and sky gods, such as the Germanic god of war Týr which is incorporated in Roman mythology as Mars. By piercing and cutting into the Earth (and terrestrial materials), it is mainly a masculine object, symbolising the Earth's marriage with and fertilisation by Heaven. In the hands of Shiva, however, axes become a symbol of fury and destruction. Ronnberg and Martin (2010) also mention how they signify in Tibet the severance of all negativities from the mind. Separation and good judgement are also symbolised by the Greek goddess Athena's birth from Zeus's head, after he orders his head to be cut open by a labrys, a double-headed axe, to stop his major headache. In modern times, axe also appeared in the emblem of Mussolini's National Fascist Party as fasces, signifying the totalitarian power of the far right. These multilayered and contrasting interpretations make axe represent an unavoidable duality, a dividing act as much as the dividing line between life and death.

Fire is not only one of the four elements that shape, warm, and illuminate the world to sustain life but also bring pain and death. Therefore, it has as many conflicting associations as the symbolism of axe. From sacred flame tending vestal virgins in Ancient Rome to the Holy Spirit's supernatural manifestation in the tongues of fire (Biedermann, 1996), from being the property of Greek and Polynesian gods (stolen by or for the benefit of man) to the inner fire in Buddhism which brings enlightenment (Chevalier and Gheerbrant, 1996b), fire is constantly associated with light and power that penetrates the mortal world. That light and power turns into punishment in the story of Lucifer, in the descriptions of eternal flames of Hell, or in Prometheus's condemnation and torment for defying the Olympian gods and stealing fire from them. Fire's destruction and negative aspects also originate from lightning bolts and volcanic eruptions that shake human foundations and reduce everything in its way to ashes. Because of this ambivalent nature, fire is sometimes associated with trickster deities (like Loki in Norse myths) which cannot be fully trusted and is mostly seen as a male element as opposed to water, which is considered female. Fire is directly connected to heart, mind/intellect, sexual potency, and desires (as in kundalini fire). Its destructive power is also seen as purifying, connected to the symbols of renewal and rebirth (as in phoenix), and is an important component of firewalking (pyrobasia) rituals observed in different parts of the world. Plus, in alchemy, fire is symbolised by a triangle which connects it visually to the blade on an axe, bringing life and death together in a masculine context again.

These two symbols, with their deeply embedded connections to life and death situations, enrich these films' murder narratives during the scenes they appear in. When Jack picks up the axe in *The Shining*, it is clear that he will not use it to cut wood but to chop up Wendy and Danny. During the famous bathroom scene that follows where his wife and son are trapped and screaming, he smashes his way through the door with the same axe, representing his fury and maleficent dominance over their lives, determined not only to end his marriage but also separate his family's physical existence from this world. Focusing only on destruction and nothing else, he freezes to death in the maze still clutching the iron tool, indicating that this masculine object of power he relentlessly holds on to is also capable of leading him to his own demise. In *Doctor Sleep*, a similar axe appears when Dan, now partially possessed by the hotel's evil forces, goes after Abra and attempts to kill her, following the same path of his destructive father (at least until he gains control over his urge to kill). On the other hand, during the barn scene in *Flickan som lekte med elden*, this masculine symbol is used by a woman, this time to end the life of a man. Zalachenko and his unceasing hatred towards any and every woman face the axe literally, now wielded by his own daughter and determined to bring final judgement upon his heinous crimes.

The destructive and punishing power of fire is also a shared narrative in these films. When Lisbeth is first introduced in *Män som hatar kvinnor*, the film shows a snippet of her memory of burning her father through a dream sequence from which she wakes up sweaty and disturbed. This memory is fully shown towards the end of the film (117:05) (and repeated in the sequel at 78:05). She runs towards Zalachenko's car with a milk carton full of gasoline. She douses him with it, lights a match, throws it at the shocked man sitting at the wheel, and turns him into a living human torch. To conceal a Soviet defector's existence in the country, Swedish authorities then declare Lisbeth insane and put her in a psychiatric hospital. In the sequel, her former legal guardian Holger Palmgren (Per Oscarsson[2]) explains that, Lisbeth, then 12 years old, decided to kill her father that day after finding her mother Agneta lying unconscious on the kitchen floor. He specifically makes it clear that social services should have intervened earlier because of the ongoing sexual assaults, beatings, and further domestic abuse Agneta and Lisbeth endured, but nothing happened until Lisbeth decided to kill her father in despair and with fury. Therefore, the sequel's title, which means 'the girl who played with fire', does not refer to a simple, child-like and innocent play with matches, but to a murderous rage which only punishing flames can quell. These punishing flames also appear in the first film as Lisbeth coldly watches the misogynistic serial killer Martin Vanger burn to death in his car but does not rescue him (117:46).

Doctor Sleep, on the other hand, uses fire's destructive symbolism in a more positive context. During his final battle scene with the evil forces of the Overlook, Dan decides to overload the hotel's boiler in order to make it explode. As the hotel goes up in flames, Dan is shown to reunite with his mother's spirit in a loving eternal embrace, suggesting that he has successfully subdued all of his childhood demons (including his father) that turned their lives into hell, and the mother and the child have nothing to fear anymore. Flanagan also depicts Abra watching the hotel burn down in a short scene which resembles the sequence where Lisbeth watches Martin burn. Abra stares at the Overlook as the fire purifies the evil trapped in the building (which she likens to cancer), hoping she can start a new life without any threat from them.

With their rich imagery and complex narratives, these films look at one of the most taboo and traumatic subjects in cinema: the hatred between a father and a child which leads both of them to death and destruction. This hatred can run so deep that it might be impossible to mend what is broken, and the only solution that presents itself for this unsustainable conflict can appear as murder. The next section will explore some of the academic perspectives regarding the problem of filicide and patricide and how these films depict this problem.

Unwanted children and bigoted fathers: the tragedy of domestic homicide

From a psychoanalytic perspective, Royston (2006) argued that analysts generally ask an important question when it comes to murder: what part of the murderer was also killed in the body of the other? This is because, he noted, the other person represented a part of the assailant's own personality – a part which they intensely disliked, or sometimes feared. In other words, Royston pointed out a clear psychoanalytical position where acts of aggression and destructiveness are also intertwined with projection, self-aggrandisement, and self-glorification.

The National Family Violence Surveys conducted in 1975 and 1985 in the United States showed that roughly a quarter of all murders took place between relatives, and most often between spouses (Straus and Gelles, 1986). Again, in the United States, between 1977 and 1986 more than 300 children killed their parents (Heide, 1992a). A review in Quebec, Canada found that parricide accounted for nine per cent of all domestic homicides that were recorded between 1990 and 2005 (Bourget et al., 2007). Similarly, an Australian study showed that parricide constituted twelve percent of all recorded domestic homicides in the country (Bryant and Cussen, 2015). On the other hand, Holt's (2017) extensive study covering England and Wales showed that between 1977 and 2012 parricide amounted to three percent of all homicides, with fathers of white ethnicity forming the largest victim group, and the use of sharp instrument being the most frequent method of killing. FBI records in the United States also indicate a statistical increase in family homicides between 2005 and 2013 (Federal Bureau of Investigation, 2016).

In her book called *Why Kids Kill Parents*, Heide (1992b) put adolescent parricide offenders into three categories based on the reason behind the murder: abuse; mental illness; and antisocial personality. She later expanded on this perspective by suggesting that mental illness plays a bigger part in adult parricide offences, and abuse is a more common reason for adolescent offences (Heide, 2013). Holt (2017) points out that killing a parent after years of childhood abuse can appear to other people as a terrible but rational motive for murder which makes Royston's psychoanalytic perspective questionable (especially from a judicial perspective) as these offenders are not destroying a part of themselves in the body of their parents, but they rather aim to stop the abuse they are suffering at the hands of their parents.

When a child kills their parent, this murder becomes a subcategory of domestic/family violence, even though findings suggest that they are two distinct crimes (Walsh and Krienert, 2009). Child-to-parent violence, a seriously under-researched area on its own, is also frequently linked with studies in childhood aggression and juvenile delinquency (Rutter, 2023). Being a multilayered problem, it is also heavily stigmatised and, for example as in the UK, justice and law enforcement policies may fail to include this phenomenon explicitly (Condry and Miles, 2014). The existing – but insufficient – literature on parricide has gaps of knowledge, limited evidence, mostly anecdotal information, and therefore can present inconclusive results. Comparative studies, on the other hand, indicate that murders are typically committed in the same houses where children and the victims, namely their parents, live together (Bourget et al., 2007; Walsh and Krienert, 2007; Heide, 2014), and children often resort to extreme violence for their murderous act (Weisman and Sharma, 1997), probably due to the deep helplessness they feel, especially if it is related to parental abuse. As a rare insight, Singhal and Dutta's (1990) study gave voice to ten men who killed their fathers. They described their fathers as punitive, shaming parents who favoured other siblings, and they were also reported to have exhibited a sense of relief rather than remorse following murder.

When it comes to filicide, Schwartz and Isser (2012) describe children as an endangered species, and how they are seen and treated throughout history. Mentioning the killings of infants (such as the biblical story of Moses, and the writings from the Han dynasty era in China), they note that many different reasons such as religious sacrifice, superstition, fear of punishment, or simply birth control play a part in parents' path to murder. In Roman law and tradition, *pater familias* (father of the family) was the oldest male in the family who had legal authority over the family property as well as his dependants, and he held the ancient right of life and death. Meaning, every child was subjected to the will of the father, and they could be swiftly disposed of – for example, killed (if they were physically deformed) or sold as a slave. The will of the mother simply did not exist. On the other hand, *Medea*, the famous Greek play by Euripides, showed not only that a jealous wife can turn into a murderer and kill her own children to punish her husband but also made a literary text timeless as it explored the darkest corners of human morality. Child murder remained in existence throughout the Middle Ages (Kellum, 1974) despite prevalent religious restrictions and other attempts to deny or cover up its continuation. It was only after the introduction of new laws in England and France during the sixteenth and seventeenth centuries that filicide became a crime punishable by death (West, 2007; Peza, 2023). Further legal developments similar to England's Infanticide Acts in 1922 and 1938 were later adopted in other Western states.

Filicide appears as the umbrella term describing any murder of a child up to the age of 18 (which includes neonaticide and infant homicide) by a parent or legal guardian. But because different scholars use different criteria and methods it is difficult to form a universal definition (Flynn et al., 2009). Also, these studies can define the age range of victims differently (for example, up to 16), and include or exclude other care givers (apart from the biological parents) as perpetrators. Because filicide is as difficult and taboo a subject as parricide/patricide, the majority of studies did not start until the late 1980s, and there are still gaps in research. However, Phillip Resnick's (1969) review of filicide cases between 1751 and 1967 (where offenders were a mix of men and women) is still one of most significant and referenced studies in this area because it provided insight into the reasons and motives behind the murder. Following these observations, Scott (1973) further focused on paternal filicide, Guileyardo et al. (1999) enhanced Resnick's classification, and Meyer et al. (2001) examined the causes of maternal filicide. Putkonen et al. (2016) also proposed a new classification system based on the recorded filicide cases in Austria and Finland between 1995 and 2005.

Even though the reasons for filicide can be complex and unique in each case, these classifications also highlighted common motives that drive people to filicide. These common reasons can be: altruistic/mercy killing (the child is murdered because the parent decides it is best for the child – for example if the child is suffering or will suffer); unwanted child; mental health problems/ psychopathology; and torture/revenge (the child is killed by one of the parents in order to harm the other). Neglect, and assault/abuse related deaths are also listed, and these reasons can sometimes share elements with unwanted child or unintentional/accidental filicide categories. While postpartum depression, and Munchausen syndrome by proxy (renamed as Factitious Disorder imposed on the child) can appear as reasons for maternal filicide, victim stimuli (meaning, the child triggers the desire to kill) appear for paternal filicide. The methods of murder differ depending on the parent. Statistically speaking, mothers prefer more head-based means such as strangulation or suffocation, whereas fathers' methods are more violent and include shooting, stabbing, or crushing. Social isolation, unemployment, poor education, personal history of abuse, or simply jealousy are listed as some of the contributing factors in filicide. It is important to note that while the vast majority of reviewed cases appear to include only heterosexual parents, filicide can also occur in same-sex couple households (Goldberg, 2024). All of these studies show that murder, either in the form of parricide or filicide, becomes the very last act in a relationship between a parent and a child. This destructive and harrowing finale to what is expected to be a mutually loving, warm, and supportive bond is not only shocking to other people but also enormously difficult to untangle and decode for researchers.

The sequelised narratives of Danny and Lisbeth come together in this challenging and blood-soaked context. In *The Shining*, as Jack Torrence runs after Danny into the hedge maze still holding his axe and screaming Danny's name, he is depicted as the father who has completely lost his love and compassion towards his son. Whatever is left of his humanity gradually dissolves in his desire to kill, and he is reduced from a man to an animal-like being which is only capable of howling and grunting, even unable to pronounce his son's name. Of course, Jack's situation is suggested to be the result of the Overlook's evil influence on him. In other words, maybe if he had not taken the job of being the caretaker, he would not have been possessed by the hotel's malevolent forces. In *Doctor Sleep*, however, Jack's spirit reappears and discloses an interesting personal detail which shines a new light on his filicide attempt.

In this crucial scene (121:29) (in the Director's Cut version, 146:00), Jack looks calm and dapper, with a deep red velvet jacket and a black bow tie. He pours Danny a glass of whiskey, sinisterly aware that this might bring his son's alcohol addiction back. While Danny tells him that he remembers Jack's whiskey bottles at home and how they smelled like fire, Jack insists that his name is Lloyd and Danny is confusing him with somebody else. As Danny refuses to take the bait and drink, he continues to explain in tears how he and his mother were traumatised and how they grieved for years. This leads to Jack gradually revealing what he thought and how he felt about his wife and son at the time. He first describes alcohol as medicine, a liquid cure for anything that troubles the soul such as depression, remorse, or failure, because it erases them from the mind, at least for a while. Then he paints in words how a man can become surrounded, disillusioned, and trapped by his family's mouths, constantly eating, crying, screaming or nagging, even though that man is trying his best to provide. He says that a family devours a man's soul, that it is enough to make a man sick, and therefore his only medicine is alcohol.

This heartbreaking description indicates that Jack was not really possessed. He deeply resented Wendy and Danny all along, and he saw them as mouths trying to eat him alive. The hotel, or in fact alcohol, did not really compel him to do anything he was not capable of doing. What alcohol did was simply to bring out what was already inside him: a self-pitying man with an endless hate towards his family who only has the courage to kill them when he is drunk. The medicine he describes not only wipes out his fears and inhibitions but also enables him to try and wipe his family out of existence. In other words, Jack reveals to Danny that the reason behind his filicide attempt was him seeing Danny as an unwanted child in an unwanted family.

Being an unwanted child is also the sad fate of Lisbeth Salander. However, what complicates Lisbeth's position is the unshakable misogyny of her father. As described earlier, Lisbeth and Zalachenko's reunion scene in the sequel (104:10) prove that their intense dislike for each other has not diminished in all those years, only deepened. As Zalachenko describes how he saw Lisbeth's mother Agneta as a whore, he also says he still hates Lisbeth. He then insults her by describing Bjurmann as a man who has no taste in women just because he raped Lisbeth. The palpable hatred in this scene goes both ways. As the father frankly reveals how worthless she is to him compared to her half-brother who Zalachenko specifically trained as a hitman, the daughter also makes it obvious how glad she is for the permanent scars she has given him. Therefore, the film establishes Lisbeth as not only an unwanted child but also a hated one just because she is female and shows that her attempted patricide in order to avenge the abuse she and her mother endured paves the way for Zalachenko's revenge.

Jack Torrence and Alexander Zalachenko are not the only two unsympathetic and hostile fathers depicted in these films. *Män som hatar kvinnor* delivers a complete, unblinking patricide scene through the memories of Harriet Vanger. After a tearful reunion with her uncle Henrik, she reveals (133:15) that her father started raping her when she reached the age of 14. A year later, her father takes her to his cottage for further sexual abuse and brings her brother Martin along to teach him how to rape. One day, now bruised, bleeding, and fed up with the abuse, Harriet decides to escape barefoot and runs to their small boat. Her drunk father, staggering and reciting many verses from the Bible (and boasting about the number of women he has killed so far), comes after her with a determination to punish her disobedience. Harriet takes an oar from the boat, hits him hard to knock him unconscious, then pushes him underwater until he is drowned.[3] She makes it look like an accident, but her brother Martin sees her efforts, and therefore Harriet's new and worse cycle of abuse begins – until she comes up with a disappearance plan and runs away from her family. As Harriet tells this story years later – and confesses the murder – the camera focuses mainly on her face. She does not cry. She is, quite understandably, in a pensive mood. She sometimes looks away with the burden of her memories. But what is interesting in this scene is that Harriet, without being schizophrenic or having a personality-disorder, provides an alternative and thought-provoking perspective to Singhal and Dutta's (1990) study when she describes her father as a punitive man who favoured her sibling: the link between hatred of women and patricide. Following years of abuse, she does not exhibit a sense of remorse, but only a sense of relief knowing that the man she knew as her father cannot hurt her anymore.

Florence (1995) skilfully points out that while the myths of the Western world include many examples of conflict and murder between fathers and sons, it is not possible to find a myth that depicts a daughter killing her father. She argues that while the conventional patriarchy justifies (or sometimes even legitimises) the power struggle between men, women killing their fathers appear outside reality, as something inconceivable, insane, or ridiculous. Several sociological studies on girl violence (Artz, 1998; Brown, 2003; Morash and Chesney-Lind, 2009), on the other hand, indicate that girls' physical aggression stems from an anger at men's and boys' dominance and control over their bodies and sexuality. The so-called 'woman's place' within a strict, gendered, and hierarchical social system contribute to feelings of powerlessness, and when coupled with being on the receiving end of abuse, homicide appears as the last resort for several female offenders (Heide, 2003; Peterson, 1999). Within this context, in Lisbeth and Harriet's cases, it is evident that their fathers' misogyny and religion-fuelled bigotry pushed both girls to commit patricide.

Every type of domestic homicide is a tragedy, causing immense suffering which is almost always impossible to put into words. When it comes to fathers killing their children (or children killing their fathers), the act becomes a bigger unspoken taboo. But this family catastrophe, the extreme horror of this experience (alongside the pain and deep sorrow it causes) does not simply go away, and it becomes a part of both the individual and the collective psyche. The next section will explore some of the Jungian perspectives of this deadly father–child dynamic.

Destinies and inheritances: the daemonic father's destruction

One of Jung's most frequently quoted perspectives on crime and human nature appears in Volume 10 of his Collected Works. Jung, leaving nothing to interpretation, wrote clearly that human nature makes everybody a potential criminal (CW 10, para. 572). In his rather enigmatically titled essay called 'The Significance of the Father in the Destiny of the Individual' (Jung, 1961), he also pointed out how individual fathers inevitably embody the father archetype as a whole, with its light and shadow, and that is why people universally agree that the father is both a divine and a daemonic figure (CW 4, para. 744). Quoting the Book of Job in the Old Testament, he described the Heavenly Father as both a creator and a destroyer (CW 5, para. 89), a paternal figure of omnipotence and unforgiving persecution.

This dual nature of fathers has been present in other texts as well. Preceding the teachings of the Old Testament, Greek and Roman myths depict the cyclical and transgenerational conflicts between fathers and their offspring since the beginning of time. As mentioned at the beginning of this chapter, Gaia, the primordial mother, persuades Cronus, her son, to attack his father Uranus. Cronus (in Roman mythology, Saturn) takes the throne after defeating his father, and gets dethroned by his son Zeus (Jupiter) after a bloody ten-year war. In these myths, the conflict develops after the father becomes power-hungry and tyrannical, highlighting that the source of creation and destruction, good and evil is in one and the same male god.

Jung referred to these stories of patricide and filicide several times in his *Collected Works*, including the legend of Ixion who killed his father-in-law (CW 5, p. 303), and the tale of Abraham and Isaac which he thinks set a bad example for people because it linked authority/supremacy with cruelty (CW

11, para. 661). For Jung, destruction is inevitably associated with the fixation with power. In his *Two Essays on Analytical Psychology*, he argues that love and power do not reign together (CW 7, para. 78). Meaning, when the desire for power, the drive to rule is predominant, there is no room for love. Power without love can only lead to violent endings which are then inherited by offsprings and start another cycle of destruction.

Apart from myths and legends, Jung included a few (but brief) real-life examples of fathers being slain by their children. However, he did not elaborate on them under a focused heading such as patricide. These children, Jung wrote, were either mentally 'defective' (he used the term 'backward children' to describe them; CW 17, para. 131) or psychopathic. The 'backward' boy who killed his stepfather at the age of fourteen with an axe (CW 17, para. 133), and the psychopathic boy who tried to murder his father at the age of nine (CW 17, para. 136) are two of his brief observations regarding this family horror without further elaboration.

As explored in the previous section, contemporary research points out that reasons like mental deficiencies or psychopathology do not present the whole picture when it comes to patricide. On the contrary, they seem to reduce the complexity into a simplified category. Children, adolescents, and sometimes adults do react violently to violent and abusive parents. As the old saying goes, violence begets violence. If a father truly plays a part in the destiny of the individual, an oppressive, ruthless, or a sadistic father can only manifest destruction – either in the form of a damaged child who can cause harm to themselves or others, or a vengeful child who is hell-bent on getting even in the most bitter way.

Jung's archetypal perspectives also led to the emergence of research and modern applications in psychology. The Myers–Briggs Type Indicator (Myers, 1962) and the Pearson–Marr Archetype Indicator (Pearson and Marr, 2003) are two well-known examples where archetypes are linked with psychological types of individuals. When it comes to parents, the antonymic positioning of the Caregiver and the Destroyer archetype highlights the light-dark duality once more. Willing to provide care, and being full of love, kindness and compassion are some of the qualities listed for the Caregiver archetype. Their focus is outwardly, aiming to create safe and nurturing spaces for others to thrive. The Destroyer archetype, on the other hand, embodies the capacity of causing harm, both to self and others, with an out-of-control hatred or anger which eventually causes their own destruction. The Destroyer personifies all addictions, compulsions, and destructive behaviours, such as emotional/physical abuse, rape, and murder. Therefore, a father can easily be a nurturing caregiver for their children, or simply a homicidal serial rapist.

Similar to the situation in other fields of research such as criminology or violence studies, patricide and filicide are neither popular nor extensively discussed and researched topics among post-Jungians. When it is discussed, the focus is frequently on the symbolism of this act and its contents, mainly coming from the angle of generational gaps and the old ways of thinking versus the new. For example, Tacey (1997, p. 45), quoting Hillman, wrote that the child (they used the gendered word 'son' instead) does not *need* to kill the father, but can *redeem* him. Looking at the horror stories of Danny, Lisbeth, and Harriet, this might sound like an incurably romantic statement with a dash of wishful thinking. How can these abused children compensate for the defects of their fathers? How can they make amends for their fathers' violence? Can they declare them innocent, or save their fathers from evil? If fathers are significant in the destiny of the individual, what sort of reparation or atonement is destined for or inherited by these children? How can Danny redeem his angry alcoholic father who thinks his son is devouring his soul and therefore must be murdered? How can Lisbeth or Harriet redeem their fathers who think they are and will always be worthless, secondary, or subservient to men, just because they are female? How can they trump a homicidal father?

These children are trapped, both physically and psychologically, with a father who abandoned his caregiving role and embodied instead, in Jungian terms, the daemonic figure of corrupt and despotic omnipotence which turned them into a murderer. Therefore, these fathers' filicide is counterbalanced by their children's patricide. Just like several real-life offenders, their answer to their unceasing, unrepentant paternal abuse is just as violent. When Danny finally blows up the hotel, he not only destroys its physical form but also puts an end to the enduring malignancy of his father, a hostility which haunted him for years and which is now just another face of the Overlook's evil. When Lisbeth burns her father, she does it with the anger and frustration of seeing the only caregiver she knew harmed carelessly and repeatedly by him. When Harriet drowns her father, it becomes an act of self-defence. In these stories, the generational conflict takes the form of domestic homicide, violence begets violence, and destruction becomes a destiny, an unwelcome inheritance for these children.

Where is the redemption for these fathers? Is there any? Maybe this question is flawed. Rather than focusing on redeeming the fathers, the question can be reframed: how did these children play the hand they were dealt? What have they achieved? Danny, Lisbeth, and Harriet stopped murderers who – unfortunately – happened to be their fathers. They made sure that these people would not and could not hurt them or anybody else ever again. Of course, this incredibly heavy burden of standing their ground against parental violence makes them tragic heroes. Danny dies, Lisbeth is left fighting for her life, and Harriet had to spend all her adult life in hiding and traumatised. However, Danny dies in order to destroy the Overlook where his impenitent father's spirit happily resides. With this sacrifice, he saves Abra and helps her live the childhood he never had, knowing she would fight evil and not hide away in alcohol like he did. Lisbeth wounds her father with the axe and leaves him bleeding on the floor unconscious and helpless, probably the way he left her mother years ago, knowing her father would not have the means to train another hitman to kill anyone, including her and her friends. Harriet, in her cruelly abused state and without the help of an adult, stops a misogynistic serial killer from killing more women. In other words, they are forced to deliver retributive justice in a situation where the moral order is completely out of balance.

For Tacey and Hillman, the road to redemption, the way children can redeem their fathers appears as *surpassing* the father. Meaning, being better and greater than their fathers in such a way the older generation's errors or shortcomings are rectified, converted into good, possibly (and hopefully) for the benefit of all. In a domestic homicide context, this sentiment leads into a discussion on the fundamental nature of justice, how to stop a hostile and unforgiving power, and how to restore that moral order which is indispensable for children and their future.

Hollis (1994) notes that justice is the force all bullies, bigots, tyrants, and even gods fear. Jung's viewpoint on the link between deliberate infliction of harm and justice is also in his writings. He argues very clearly that evil causes evil in return, and even benevolent and innocent people who are pushed to being a victim due to no fault of their own can become so wrathful they can finally deliver the punishment for the wicked, commanded by fate like a sword (CW 10, para. 410). Therefore, in Jungian terms, these children committed an unavoidable crime that not only delivered punishment for but also destroyed their daemonic fathers – fathers who never loved them, fathers who never wanted them, fathers who thought they were superior to them all the way to the bitter end. If a father has any significance in the destiny of an individual, delivering justice but also becoming an offender at the same time is certainly the most traumatic and the saddest destiny for a child.

From the murderer to the grey mentor

Indifferent and absent father. Present but manipulative father. Cruel and abusive father. Out-of-control and homicidal father. They are all called fathers, but they are varieties, examples, parts of a bigger archetypal pattern. They are all but shadows of the loving, nurturing, caring father where that love, care, and support do not exist. Instead, filling that absence is either apathy or an unflinching desire for power in order to rule, to control, to own, to kill.

The penultimate chapter of this book will look at a different type of father in the shadows. A father who knows about the evils of the world and becomes a mentor to his child – but not necessarily with the desire to control, manipulate, or abuse. Blurring the lines between light and dark, this father blends in with the grey area and acts like an advisor, a guide into the shadows of human nature, a figure who is ethically questionable, if not controversial. The last stop in this exploration of fatherhood is the grey mentor.

Notes

1 The actual method of Zeus is not known. In some texts, Kronos was imprisoned after a big war, and in others Zeus castrated Kronos and sentenced him to the same fate of his grandfather Uranus.
2 A destructive, unfortunate, and sad connection with fire also appears in the death of Oscarsson. Following this role in the trilogy, the actor tragically perished in 2010 with his wife, Kia Östling, when a fire broke out in their home and burned everything to the ground.
3 Harriet's method of patricide appears in contrast with Lisbeth's. While Lisbeth uses fire, the element which is symbolically considered to be male, Harriet uses water, the element which is considered female. This contrast fits in with how these two women are portrayed as well. Lisbeth, with her short hair, tattoos, piercings, martial arts training, and bisexual affairs is presented with a masculine flair, whereas Harriet is depicted as sensitive, delicate, and graceful with long hair, precious jewellery, and creamy-coloured pastel dresses.

References

Filmography

Case 39. (2009) Directed by C. Alvart. Canada, USA.
Doctor Sleep. (2019) Directed by M. Flanagan. USA.
Flickan som lekte med elden. (2009) Directed by D. Alfredson. Denmark, Sweden.
Guardians of the Galaxy Vol. 2. (2017) Directed by J. Gunn. USA.
Joe. (1970) Directed by J. Avildsen. USA.
Män som hatar kvinnor. (2009) Directed by N. A. Oplev. Denmark, Sweden.
Murdered by My Father. (2016) Directed by B. Goodison. UK.
The Omen. (1976) Directed by R. Donner. UK, USA.
The Ring. (2002) Directed by G. Verbinski. USA.
The Shining. (1980) Directed by S. Kubrick. UK, USA.
Titus. (1999) Directed by J. Taymor. Italy, UK, USA.

Bibliography

Artz, S. (1998) 'Where have all the school girls gone? Violent girls in the school yard', *Child & Youth Care Forum*, 27(2), 77–109.
Australian Institute of Health and Welfare. (2019) *Family, Domestic and Sexual Violence in Australia: Continuing the National Story.* Canberra: Australian Institute of Health and Welfare. https://doi.org/10.25816/5ebcc837fa7ea.
Biedermann, H. (1996) 'Fire', in *The Wordsworth Dictionary of Symbolism.* Ware: Wordsworth Editions.
Brown, M. L. (2003) *Girlfighting: Betrayal and Rejection among Girls.* New York: New York University Press.
Bourget, D., Gagné, P. and Labelle, M. E. (2007) 'Parricide: a comparative study of matricide versus patricide', *Journal of the American Academy of Psychiatry and the Law Online*, 35(3), 306–312.
Bryant, W. and Cussen, T. (2015) *Homicide in Australia: 2010–11 to 2011–12: National Homicide Monitoring Program Report.* Canberra: Australian Institute

of Criminology. Available at: www.aic.gov.au/media_library/publications/mr/m
r23/mr23.pdf.

Chevalier, J. and Gheerbrant, A. (1996a) 'Axe', in *The Penguin Dictionary of Symbols*.
London: Penguin.

Chevalier, J. and Gheerbrant, A. (1996b) 'Fire', in *The Penguin Dictionary of Symbols*.
London: Penguin.

Collis, C. (2019) 'Stephen King says Doctor Sleep film "redeems" Stanley Kubrick's
The Shining', available at: www.ew.com/movies/2019/11/05/stephen-king-doctor-
sleep-redeems-the-shining-stanley-kubrick/.

Condry, R. and Miles, C. (2014) 'Adolescent to parent violence: Framing and mapping
a hidden problem', *Criminology & Criminal Justice*, 14(3), 257–275.

Federal Bureau of Investigation. (2016) 'Uniform crime reports', available at: www.fbi.
gov/about-us/cjis/ucr/crime-in-the-u.s/.

Florence, P. (1995) 'The daughter's patricide', *European Journal of Women's Studies*, 2,
185–203.

Flynn, S., Windfuhr, K. and Shaw, J. (2009) *Filicide: A Literature Review*. The
National Confidential Inquiry into Suicide and Homicide by People with Mental
Illness Centre for Suicide Prevention. Manchester: University of Manchester.
Available at: https://documents.manchester.ac.uk/display.aspx?DocID=37579.

Goldberg, A. E. (2024) 'LGBTQ parents and filicide: Focus on the Hart Family murders', in A. E. Goldberg, D. C. Slakoff, and C. L. Buist (eds) *The (Mis)Repre-
sentation of Queer Lives in True Crime*. New York: Routledge, pp. 256–276.

Guileyardo, J. M., Prahlow, J. A., and Barnard, J. J. (1999) 'Familial filicide and filicide classification', *The American Journal of Forensic Medicine and Pathology*, 20
(3), 286–292.

Heide, K. M. (1992a) 'Why kids kill parents: How a legacy of child abuse leads to
homicide', *Psychology Today*, 25(5), 62–77.

Heide, K. M. (1992b) *Why Kids Kill Parents: Child Abuse and Adolescent Homicide*.
Columbus: Ohio State University Press.

Heide, K. M. (2003) 'Youth homicide: A review of the literature and a blueprint for
action', *International Journal of Offender Therapy & Comparative Criminology*, 47,
6–36.

Heide, K. M. (2013) *Understanding Parricide: When Sons and Daughters Kill Parents*.
Oxford: Oxford University Press.

Heide, K. M. (2014) 'Patricide and steppatricide victims and offenders: an empirical
analysis of US arrest data', *International Journal of Offender Therapy and Comparative Criminology*, 58(11), 1261–1278.

Hollis, J. (1994) *Under Saturn's Shadow: The Wounding and Healing of Men*. Toronto:
Inner City Books.

Holt, A. (2017) 'Parricide in England and Wales (1977–2012): An exploration of
offenders, victims, incidents and outcomes', *Criminology & Criminal Justice*, 17(5),
568–587.

Jung, C. G. (1960) *The Collected Works of C. G. Jung, Volume 3: The Psychogenesis
of Mental Disease*. Princeton: Princeton University Press.

Jung, C. G. (1961) *The Collected Works of C. G. Jung, Volume 4: Freud & Psychoanalysis*. Princeton: Princeton University Press.

Jung, C. G. (1967) *The Collected Works of C. G. Jung, Volume 5: Symbols of Transformation*. Princeton: Princeton University Press.

Jung, C. G. (1967) *The Collected Works of C. G. Jung, Volume 7: Two Essays on Analytical Psychology.* Princeton: Princeton University Press.

Jung, C. G. (1970) *The Collected Works of C. G. Jung, Volume 10: Civilization in Transition.* Princeton: Princeton University Press.

Jung, C. G. (1970) *The Collected Works of C. G. Jung, Volume 11: Psychology and Religion: West and East.* Princeton: Princeton University Press.

Jung, C. G. (1954) *The Collected Works of C. G. Jung, Volume 17: The Development of Personality.* Princeton: Princeton University Press.

Kellum, B. A. (1974) 'Infanticide in England in the later Middle Ages', *The Journal of Psychohistory*, 1(3), 367.

King, S. (1974) *Carrie.* New York: Doubleday.

King, S. (1977) *The Shining.* New York: Doubleday.

King, S. (2013) *Doctor Sleep.* New York: Scribner.

Larsson, S. (2005) *Män som hatar kvinnor.* Stockholm: Norstedts Förlag.

Larsson, S. (2006) *Flickan som lekte med elden.* Stockholm: Norstedts Förlag.

Larsson, S. (2007) *Luftslottet som sprängdes.* Stockholm: Norstedts Förlag.

Liem M., Levin, J., Holland, C., and Fox, J. A. (2013) 'The nature and prevalence of familicide in the United States, 2000–2009', *Journal of Family Violence*, 28(4), 351–358. https://doi.org/10.1007/s10896-013-9504-2.

Meyer, C. L., Oberman, M., and White, K. (2001) *Mothers Who Kill Their Children: Understanding the Acts of Moms from Susan Smith to the 'Prom Mom'.* New York: New York University Press.

Morash, M. AndChesney-Lind, M. (2009) 'Girls' violence in context', in M. Zahn (ed.) *The Delinquent Girl.* Philadelphia: Temple University Press, pp. 182–206.

Mouzos J. and Rushforth C. (2003) *Family Homicide in Australia.* Trends & Issues in Crime and Criminal Justice, 255. Canberra: Australian Institute of Criminology.

Myers, I. B. (1962) *The Myers-Briggs Type Indicator: Manual.* Berkeley: Consulting Psychologists Press.

Pearson, C. L. and Marr. H. K. (2003) *PMAI Manual: A Guide for Interpreting the Pearson-Marr Archetype Indicator Instrument.* Gainesville: Center for Applications of Psychological Type.

Peterson, E. (1999) 'Murder as self-help: Women and intimate partner homicide', *Homicide Studies*, 3, 30–46.

Peza, G. (2023) 'Social and Psychological Factors Related to Filicide: A Literature Review', *Beder Journal of Educational Sciences*, 26(2), 157–170. https://doi.org/10.5281/zenodo.8070104.

Putkonen, H., Amon, S., Weizmann-Henelius, G., Pankakoski, M., Eronen, M., Almiron, M. P., and Klier, C. M. (2016) 'Classifying filicide', *The International Journal of Forensic Mental Health*, 15(2), 198–210. https://doi.org/10.1080/14999013.2016.1152616.

Resnick, P. J. (1969) 'Child murder by parents: A psychiatric review of filicide', *American Journal of Psychiatry*, 126(3), 325–334.

Ronnberg, A. and Martin, K. (eds.) (2010) 'Ax', in *The Book of Symbols: Reflections on Archetypal Images.* Cologne: Taschen.

Royston, R. (2006) 'Destructiveness: revenge, dysfunction or constitutional evil?', in C. Harding (ed.) *Aggression and Destructiveness: Psychoanalytic Perspectives.* New York: Routledge, pp. 23–37.

Rutter, N. (2023) '"My [search strategies] keep missing you": A scoping review to map child-to-parent violence in childhood aggression literature', *International Journal of Environmental Research and Public Health*, 20, 4176. https://doi.org/10.3390/ijerph20054176.

Schwartz, L. L. and Isser, N. (2012) *Endangered Children: Homicide and Other Crimes*. Boca Raton: CRC Press.

Scott, P. D. (1973) 'Parents who kill their children', *Medicine, Science, and the Law*, 13 (2), 120–126.

Singhal, S. and Dutta, A. (1990) 'Who commits patricide?', *Acta Psychiatrica Scandinavica*, 82(1), 40–43.

Straus, M. A. and Gelles, R. J. (1986) 'Societal change and change in family violence from 1975 to 1985 as revealed by two national surveys', *Journal of Marriage and the Family*, 48, 465–479.

Tacey, David J. (1997) *Remaking Men: Jung, Spirituality and Social Change*. New York: Routledge.

Walsh, J. A. and Krienert, J. L. (2007) 'Child-parent violence: an empirical analysis of offender, victim, and event characteristics in a national sample of reported incidents', *Journal of Family Violence*, 22, 563–574.

Walsh, J. A. and Krienert, J. L. (2009) 'A decade of child-initiated family violence: Comparative analysis of child–parent violence and parricide examining offender, victim, and event characteristics in a national sample of reported incidents, 1995–2005', *Journal of Interpersonal Violence*, 24(9), 1450–1477.

Weisman, A. M. and Sharma, K. K. (1997) 'Forensic analysis and psycholegal implications of parricide and attempted parricide', *Journal of Forensic Sciences*, 42(6), 1107–1113.

West, S. G. (2007) 'An overview of filicide', *Psychiatry (Edgmont)*, 4(2), 48–57.

World Health Organization. (2012) *Understanding and Addressing Violence against Women*. Geneva: World Health Organization.

Chapter 5

The grey mentor

The father, according to one of Jung's dream interpretations (CW 12, paras 158–159), not only represented one's own country but also is the figure who shares the secrets of life and life's meaning based on old teachings. In other words, fathers fulfil an informing function. They impart a great deal of knowledge to their offspring. This transmission of information and wisdom between generations forms the basis of the famous Jungian archetype called the wise old man. In fact, Jung specifically stated that while Anima personified *life*, the wise old man personified *meaning* (CW 14, para. 313). Hopcke (1999) expanded on this definition by saying that wise old man is a force. According to him, this force is not phallic or penetrating (as in the hero or the father archetype), but a magical, resourceful inner strength that accompanies, helps, and directs a person when they try to navigate their struggles. A derivative of the archetypal father, wise old man is the enlightened combination of thinking and feeling, Anima and Animus, male and female, Logos and Eros, protection and nurturing. It is a combination where the experience of life leads to meaning and this 'knowledge' is passed on without being forceful or without the need/desire to command or dominate.

Wisdom is generally defined as the insight or the ability to discern what is true, right, and ethical. Unbiased judgement, non-attachment, a transformed self through the acquisition of skills and knowledge are some of the qualities of this capacity to think deeply and act productively. But the path to wisdom can take one through both virtue and vice, knowing and experiencing opposites. If everyone has a shadow, as Jung argues, does the wise old man have one too? Hopcke (1999, p. 118) answered this question and gave the example of Jung himself as described by Jung's critics: architect of a cult; self-important guru; supporter of totalitarian views. While these descriptions are beyond the discussion of this book, the questions remain: what happens when fathers (or father figures) carry the burden of wisdom, of knowing what is good and what is bad? How would they pass on this knowledge to their children? What is hiding in the shadows of this figure who is neither black nor white, but simply a grey mentor?

This chapter travels through these questions with the help of the crafty and interesting narratives of *The Accountant* (2016) and *Bloodline* (2018). While

DOI: 10.4324/9781003394488-5

the former explores autism and the lengths a father would go to teach his son how to survive, and the latter is a gory look at the double life of a social worker who provides counselling to abused teenagers and removes the source of abuse from their lives discreetly. The next section will tell the story of a mathematical genius who was abandoned by his mother and raised by his brutally honest father.

Adapt or die: autism and choosing not to be a victim

The scene (49:55) starts with the word 'again'. Two boys, Braxton (Jake Presley) and Christian (Seth Lee), are grunting and fighting an adult male who is a Pencak Silat master (Ron Yuan). The boys attack the man with all their might, punches, kicks, and body blows. The master blocks all the punches swiftly and throws Braxton at Christian like a sack of potatoes. He almost immediately regains his composure and says 'again' while the two breathless boys try to stand up and get ready to attack. Braxton checks if Christian is alright. The master hits Braxton again, and the trio is back into fighting mode. The boys' father (Robert C. Treveiler) watches them from a distance calmly, quietly. He is reading a newspaper, occasionally looking at the fight in front of him. The master punches Christian off-screen and the boy falls on the ground. Braxton jumps on the back of the master with anger, only to be thrown to the ground next to his brother. Christian suddenly springs into action, attacks the master only to be punched back to the ground.

The boys are now exhausted and unable to stand up. The master turns to the father and says 'enough'. The father takes another look at his sons and disagrees. The master tries to reason with the father, saying the boys have done their best for today and they can continue their training tomorrow. The father, without a hint of emotion in his voice, responds. He says that the boys have not done their best. Because, he adds, if they had the trainer would have been covered in blood and snot instead of his sons. He coldly orders the trainer to resume the training. The trainer does not move. The father does not take this defiance well. His short monologue starts. The father argues that if aggression can be correctly channelled, it can help a person overcome a lot of flaws. He kneels in front of Christian who is rocking back and forth while he wipes away the blood running down his nose. The father looks at his son and says accessing that deep inner aggression in every human being requires peeling back several layers of personality. He adds that it is his responsibility as a father to know his sons' limits. He orders Christian to get up. He then looks at the master and says it is the master's job to peel away those layers. The trainer looks serious, and this time he does not disobey. Braxton, with a concerned look on his face, waits for his rocking brother to get up. Christian stands up, still bleeding. He then speaks in Indonesian and, without a full eye contact with the master, says he can carry on with his training.

Another flashback scene (80:59). A grey car in a rough neighbourhood. On concrete walls, one can see several graffiti, some big and coloured letters, some short and hastily scribbled. It is raining really hard – maybe it is the Monsoon season, who knows. The water makes the neighbourhood look more dismal and helpless. It is the domain of the colour grey, from the surrounding concrete to that parked car. Easy to blend in, easy to stay unnoticed, easy to survive. There was probably a jungle here, many many years ago. It was once full of vibrant colours – deep greens, blood reds, enticing purples. And now, many many years later, that jungle is replaced with a concrete one with its oppressive grey.

Three people in that grey car. The same father and his two boys. The boys are sitting in the back. Braxton is looking apprehensive. The other boy, the one who wears glasses and whose name is Christian, is looking out of the rear window, tapping restless fingers on the seat. He is not rocking back and forth anymore. He has a calm face which seems out of tune with his inner restlessness. The father starts speaking. Slowly, calmly, with carefully chosen words. He explains the probability first. The four boys waiting for his sons by the corner are most probably right-handed, and he would snap their wrists if it was up to him. Then an important life lesson begins. In an uncompromisingly forthright way, he explains how life is a series of old choices, always learned fresh by each new generation. According to him, the oldest choice is between being a victim or not. The second one, he says, is being loyal to one's family, through both the good and bad times. He continues with a weary face – it is wrong to think that people would like others who do not fight back. Being different will make people afraid of you sooner or later, he adds. He bluntly finishes his lesson: make your choice. Are you going to be a victim or not?

The restless boy with the glasses steps out of the car. He walks towards cheering boys standing on wet concrete. He approaches the tallest one and punches him straight in the face without any hesitation or fear. The other boy in the car is waiting for his father's instruction, still apprehensive. As the father says go, Braxton jumps out of the car and runs towards the fight, determined to join in and help his brother. The father stays in the car. Watching, with a stern face, the blood-splattered masculine ballet performed in front of him.

These two crucial flashback scenes are from *The Accountant* (2016). Written by Bill Dubuque and directed by Gavin O'Connor, the film tells the story of Christian Wolff (Ben Affleck), who leads a criminal life while being a certified public accountant. *The Accountant*, with its interesting take on autism, handles a complex narrative especially blurring the line between good and bad as well as strict and thoughtful parenting. Theatrically released in October 2016, the film grossed over US$155 million worldwide with a budget of US$44 million and received mixed criticisms due to its deliberate and unconventional mix of crime, violence, and neurodevelopmental disorder. In January 2024, it was announced that a sequel for the film is now in pre-production and the preparation for a third film is also under way.

Abandoned by their own mother (Mary Kraft) during a Christmas period because of Christian's continuous sensory and behavioural differences, young Braxton and Christian were raised by their father who was in the army and who refused the help of Harbor Neuroscience Center director (Jason Davis) years ago. Trained to be an efficient killer by his father's methodical teaching and learned the best ways of money laundering from a former mafia bookkeeper named Francis Silverberg (Jeffrey Tabor) while both were jailed, Christian Wolff now owns his own small business called ZZZ Accounting which acts as a front for his main source of illegal income. Christian uses the names of famous mathematicians and philosophers as fake identities, and he provides tax services to ordinary people like Frank (Ron Prather) and Dolores Rice (Susan Savoie) who are struggling with their payments, helps them through the legal loopholes in the tax system and lessens their financial worries legitimately. But his main clientele consist of cartels, arms brokers, money launderers and assassins operating worldwide. The neuroscience centre director's nonverbal autistic daughter Justine (Alison Wright) acts as a broker-dealer and discreetly assists Christian. Being a math savant, Christian specifically un-cooks his clients' books and finds any missing money they were supposed to have, helping them weed out their foes and adversaries within the criminal underworld. For his outstanding services, he gets paid in gold bars, guns, cash, and priceless original artworks such as *Woman in a Parasol and Small Child on a Sunlit Hillside* by Pierre-Auguste Renoir and *Free Form* by Jackson Pollock. While he lives in a spartan house on his own, he keeps everything he values in an Airstream PanAmerica, a travel trailer hidden at a self-storage unit, ready to change location and start from scratch with a new identity anytime and every time the law enforcement starts to close in on him.

Things come to a head when the US Department of the Treasury Director Ray King (J. K. Simmons), the person Christian discreetly tipped over the years to help him arrest criminals, decides to find this elusive accountant's real identity before he retires. He blackmails one of Treasury's data analysts, Marybeth Medina (Cynthia Addai-Robinson) into cracking this case due to her non-disclosure of her juvenile record during her job application. Meanwhile, Christian is hired to audit a firm called Living Robotics where an inhouse accountant, Dana Cummings (Anna Kendrick), discovered financial irregularities. Working with Dana overnight, Christian finds that 61 million dollars have been embezzled by somebody in the firm. When Christian shares the findings with the company owner Lamar Blackburn (John Lithgow), not only his audit ends abruptly but he also discovers that hitmen are dispatched to kill him and Dana. While Justine tips King and Medina about Living Robotics, Christian rescues Dana, and discovers that Lamar is the person behind the embezzlement. When he goes to Lamar's house for revenge, he fights his way through Braxton's men who are hired to protect Lamar. The two brothers fight each other too, but they also remember their father's rule about family. As they reconcile, Christian kills Lamar and then agrees to meet Braxton to catch up. Christian sends his Jackson Pollock painting to Dana as a parting gift and leaves Illinois for a new undisclosed location with a new fake identity. Medina is promoted by King and becomes Christian's new point of contact at the Treasury, still not knowing who or where Christian really is.

The Accountant's elaborate narrative throws quite a lot into the mix. Juggling autism, crime, murder, law enforcement, and family ties, the film deliberately combines drama with wry humour, and it was a sleeper hit when it was released. Some critics complained about the way Christine and Justine's autism is depicted, pointing out the fact that autistic children or adults are not necessarily interested in or enthusiastic about criminal activities. However, some critics also praised the ways this condition are portrayed, without extra Hollywood drama or sentimentality. While it is inevitable to remember Raymond Babbitt's (Dustin Hoffman) rather victimised and exploited position as an autistic adult in *Rain Man* (1988), Dubuque's story turns this narrative upside down and makes Christian a ferocious survivor at any cost, refusing to be a victim of both his condition and the dangers the world throws at him.

Diagnostic and Statistical Manual of Mental Disorders (DSM-5-TR; American Psychiatric Association, 2022) and *International Classification of Diseases* (ICD-11; World Health Organization, 2019) do not differentiate between Autism and Asperger's anymore. Instead, they combine the two (with the addition of pervasive developmental disorder) under the title 'autism spectrum disorder'. While there are some differences in their symptomatology and diagnostic criteria, they have several similarities which help clinicians identify and diagnose autism. Two major groups of criteria in DSM-5 and ICD-11 appear as the framework for diagnosis (Yu et al., 2024; First, et al., 2021; Joon et al., 2021). These groups are social/communication challenges, and restricted/repetitive behaviours. To qualify for autism diagnosis, a person must experience difficulty (now, or have experienced in the past) in all three areas of human interaction mentioned in the first group – maintaining social and/or emotional reciprocity, nonverbal communication, and managing all types of relationships (family, friends, work etc.). For the second group, a person must meet two of four main diagnostic criteria: sensory difference; difficulty in changing fixed behaviours; limited interests which can be profound, passionate and/or atypical; repetitive behaviours which can be personal and distinctive. Additional diagnostic criteria such as tracing these difficulties back to childhood, clinical impairments such as anxiety or depression, and a clear elimination of any intellectual disability help clinicians reach sound conclusions when they aim to diagnose autism. Although this condition is labelled and diagnosed as a 'disorder', latest and ongoing research indicate that clinicians are slowly considering a different way of describing it: a natural form of human neurological variation, rather than a disability, defect, or intellectual deficiency.

The two autistic children of the film, Christian and Justine, are depicted faithfully based on these criteria. Justine is an IT savant, completely non-verbal, and she only communicates through her special computer system, using text-to-speech methods and a computerised voice which has hardly any emotional intonation. Christian, on the other hand, can recognise complex patterns and shapes (in numbers, puzzles, art etc.), is extremely neat and tidy, and has an inflexible daily routine which includes a twenty-minute sensory overload session with loud music and flashing lights to curb his sensitivity (followed by an antidepressant – 100 mg of Zoloft). He has occasional unsystematic inaccuracies and inappropriacies in his command of language – meaning, he is sometimes unable to understand idiomatic expressions or sarcasm in daily conversations and takes them literally. His repetitive behaviour of rocking back and forth when he was a child is now replaced with him tapping his fingers or simply blowing on them before he first touches an object (pens, cutlery, guns etc.). He cannot form or maintain close relationships, and he has trouble adjusting to his unexpected friendship with Dana. His most favourite (and peaceful) moments seem to be in his Airstream trailer bedroom, completely isolated from the world and its assault on his senses, listening to classical music and looking at Pollock's *Free Form*. Christian's passion for precision and order is also creatively highlighted by the famous Radiohead (2000) song, 'Everything in its Right Place', chosen as the main song for the film's first trailer.

In the documentary called *Behavioural Science* included in the Blu-Ray edition of the film, O'Connor points out, with care, perceptiveness and appreciation, that if the autism gene is eliminated then humanity would lose many great scientists, mathematicians, and musicians. He says, through his film, he wanted to celebrate this neurodiversity and greatness which continue to enrich the world. The film, according to him, is an exploration of Christian's skills, dissecting how he became this man, a creation of his father, not only generated by love but also by teaching him the necessary skills and competence to survive in a world which would not treat him with the same amount of love and care he had for him.

Dubuque's multilayered storyline specifically depicts two caring male figures who also appear as the personifications of the wise old man archetype: Christian's own father; and Francis. Christian's father, both as a military man and as a complete opposite to the absent father explored in Chapter One, is portrayed as a very strict man who trained Christian the best way he thought he could so that his autistic son could survive in a world which is simultaneously hostile and complex. Development psychologist Dr Laurie Stephens, who is also featured in the same documentary, mentions that no autistic child is the same, and this situation makes it even more difficult for parents to understand and navigate. She says brand-new parents do not know anything about the condition, have no idea what to believe, and what can help them. This set of circumstances lead these parents to rely on their own philosophical beliefs while looking after their autistic children. Within this context, Christian's father, wanting Christian to be a strong and independent person, raised him in the best way he knew so that Christian could continue to defend/protect himself even when he (or Braxton) was not around.

The portrayal of the old mafia bookkeeper Francis Silverberg follows the same pattern in the film. While the film does not make it clear why and for how long he and Christian were incarcerated, it also does not explain how they ended up sharing the same cell. The story does, however, establish that they were together for at least two years, and during this period Francis became like a father figure to Christian, not only due to the age difference but also because of Francis's methodical training. As a contrast to the strictness of Christian's own father, Francis gently teaches Christian the techniques of money laundering, loopholes in the system, and all the address and contact details of criminals he personally knows. But he also teaches Christian the necessary social skills he needs to blend in – for example, how to engage in small talk, simulate empathy, and appear friendly (classified under different headings, such as compensatory techniques, masking, or camouflaging; Alaghband-Rad et al., 2023; Cook et al., 2021; Livingston et al., 2019). In other words, Francis, similar to Christian's father, equips Christian not only with the essential skills and knowledge for survival (and making money in a world full of crime) but also helps him become more capable of making human connections and dealing with some of his neurological differences which might alienate him from other people.

It is essential to mention that neither Christian's father nor Francis behave like the fathers/father figures explored in previous chapters. While they neglected, manipulated, abused, or simply murdered their offspring or other children for their own selfish needs, these two men in *The Accountant* are depicted in a completely different way. As described earlier, Christian's father teaches him probably what he knows best as a military officer: resilience. Of course, this is not just about physical endurance or readiness for combat. It is also a mental and emotional robustness, the ability to withstand or overcome adverse conditions, not to mention hostile people. By teaching him everything he knew about guns and fighting, Christian learns how to channel his inner aggression/frustration to face his adversaries, and not become self-destructive or vulnerable. Christian learns what he can and cannot do, both physically and ethically, because his father also teaches him (with Braxton) the value of family, the importance of family ties, especially after Christian's mother leaves them all behind. Christian also learns from his father what honour and integrity are, and the value of protecting the innocent (which he specifically upholds and protects Frank, Dolores, and Dana from hitmen who are sent to kill them just to get to Christian). In other words, Christian's father teaches him, as a man, the opposites in life: how to care and how to kill.

Even though he has very few scenes, Francis appears as the sage of black money with the tenderness and patience of a loving grandfather. He calls Christian 'son' and his playful attentiveness when he is teaching Christian tips for better socialisation is a sharp contrast to how Christian's father is portrayed: solemn; pensive; stern; humourless; and in only one scene, when Christian's mother abandons them, tearful and helpless. Although the depictions of these two men are dissimilar, their attitudes are the same: sharing their knowledge and power in order to help a child/adult whom they perceive as a person who needs special care and support. Unlike Gregori in Chapter 2, they do not abuse their position of power to gain anything for themselves, and they help Christian become more self-aware of his uniqueness as well as the challenges he will be facing. In short, they accompany, help, and direct him when Christian is trying to navigate life and, in every respect, choosing not to be a victim in any situation.

The Accountant shows two men, two wise old men, teaching both good and bad, but leaving the choice of what to do with them to the pupil. They become grey mentors, training, advising, and counselling Christian about the unpleasant qualities of the world, the primitive, inferior, primal side of man's nature, the shadow that is in everyone. Their presence is of service to Christian's survival. When Christian specifically walks a path of questionable ethics, money laundering on the one hand and helping the US Treasury to catch criminals on the other, he is very much aware of what he is doing and why he is doing it. In a world where nothing is simply black and white, Christian follows the grey path his mentors placed before him and embodies the simple law of resilience: adapt or die.[1]

Resilience and its ties to criminality and mentoring are also explored in a different family context in this chapter's next film, *Bloodline*. This time a social worker, also a new father, is helping abused children at a school, not only by listening to them and offering guidance but also getting rid of their abusers swiftly and efficiently. A grisly tale of family ties, *Bloodline* focuses on the moral principles of serial killers with its unconventional and controversial narrative.

Does a happy daddy make a happy home? Exorcising the pain of the father

Costello (2002) argued that there are three types of criminals: neurotic; perverse; and psychotic. He classified acts of stealing under neurotic crimes, and deviant acts under perverse. When it comes to psychotic criminals, he wrote that they do not feel any guilt. Referring to the concept called *the pale criminal*, a term used by Nietzsche, he noted that psychotic criminals are actually 'rosy' criminals due to their lack of guilt. Compared to rosy criminals, he wrote, a pale criminal is somebody who is in pain and craving to be understood. Referring to Jung's word association tests which he used specifically in criminal cases (CW 18, para. 144), Costello stated that the complexity underneath both the criminal acts and the criminal minds implies a dual personality where a part of their soul is lacking love.

Borrowing themes from the minds (and acts) of two famous fictional serial killers, Dr Hannibal Lecter (Harris, 1988, 1999) and Dexter Morgan (Lindsay, 2005), *Bloodline* dives into the trauma-filled life of a social worker named Evan Cole (Sean William Scott) and focuses on patricide and the definitions of fatherhood. Based on a story by Will Honley, the script was co-written and further developed for the screen by Avra Fox-Lerne and Henry Jacobson who also directed the film. It was premiered at the Fantastic Fest film festival in September 2018 in Austin, Texas, with the tagline 'Fatherhood can be murder', presenting the difficult, complex, and sometimes unpleasant experience of being a father in a literally murderous context. In his interview (McGrew, 2019), Jacobson revealed that his wife was pregnant during the making of the film, and he apparently used this creative process as an outlet to express certain apprehensions about his future life as a parent.

In the same interview, he mentions the preliminary research for the film where they looked into the world of psychopaths and serial killers, and how they build their own moral universe in order to legitimise their reasons for murder. Exploring what would happen if a serial killer had a baby, Jacobson plays with the idea of the malevolence inherent in nuclear families through his film, walking a thin line between endorsing a murderer and demonstrating how ethical principles can be twisted easily to decide who lives and who dies. In another interview (Creative Screen Writing, 2019), Fox-Lerne points out the fact that families can be beautiful and horrifying at the same time, and the film builds on a perspective where a middle-class family's wish to exist and continue to pursue the American dream collides with reality and, sometimes, the necessity of murder.

After a graphic murder scene which opens the film and involves a nurse getting brutally killed while having a shower at a hospital, *Bloodline* introduces its main protagonist, Evan Cole. Evan, married to his immigrant and pregnant wife Lauren (Mariela Garriga), works at East Angeles High School with vulnerable teenagers who are either sexually or physically abused by their fathers or other older male relatives who are mainly on parole. Being a domestic violence victim himself when he was a boy, Evan offers these students the calm and supportive space to discuss their experiences and offer them counselling. Even though many students are unable to trust a stranger like Evan at first, they slowly warm to him. Especially three students, Ray (Sean H. Scully), Kelly (Larsen Thompson), and Chris (Raymond Cham Jr.), share their horrible experiences with him while crying, bleeding, or in an anxious state on the verge of self-harm.

With the birth of his own son, Evan's calm, kind, and sensitive attitude starts to crack under pressure. Caught in a vicious cycle of feeding, nappy changing, and putting his baby to sleep while being sleep deprived, his nightmarish memories of his own father's violence and how he killed him as a boy in order to protect his mother start to resurface. When his mother Marie (Dale Dickey) comes home to help the new parents (and kills the nurse Carrie (Christie Herring) at the hospital who treats all three rudely), this gives him the opportunity to release his deeply rooted anger on his students' abusers by killing them one by one. When the detective Overstreet (Kevin Carroll) recognises the connection between the murders, Evan, and the students, he warns Lauren that it is only a matter of time and Evan will be arrested as soon as they find physical evidence. To protect his family, Lauren decides to kill Chris who also realises that Evan had murdered his father. She shoots Chris with his own gun, making it look like a suicide, and posts a social media confession of other murders (as Chris) through Chris's phone. Overstreet closes the case. Evan, Lauren, and Marie continue to share the joy and the responsibility of looking after their newborn as a family of murderers in peace, at least for the time being.

The film's title, *Bloodline*, is a clever wordplay referring to both kinship/lineage and a bloody trail of dead bodies. To present the moral conundrum of the film, the director Henry Jacobson shows the core of Evan's trauma in two flashback scenes which leave nothing to the imagination. The first scene (16:07) starts in slow motion where a drunk grown man (Matthew Bellows) with a furious face, shouting the words 'you little shit', throws a punch with all his might at a little boy (Hudson West). The boy drops to the floor with the force of the punch. Because the man's body movements are hysterically furious and violent, he loses his own balance after the punch and tries to steady himself by the kitchen countertop. A young woman (Cassandra Ballard) grabs a big knife and holds it to the man's throat. She speaks with the threatening voice and tells the man to get away from the child who is bleeding and crying on the floor. Her voice changes immediately to a loving one and gently asks the child to go to his room. The man offers his apology to the woman, revealing her name, Marie. Marie replies with a cold 'get out'. The man looks at the crying boy and smiles. He asks him, addressing him as Evan, if he knows he did not mean what he said. Marie, again with a cold and determined voice, promises to kill the man if he does not leave immediately. The drunk man gives up, slowly backs off with his hands in the air, and leaves the house. Evan gets up, still crying, still bleeding. His mother holds him in her arms, starts caressing his back, calling him a sweetheart, gently telling him that everything will be alright while Evan weeps silently.

The second flashback scene appears midway through the film (56:45). This time Evan's sober father is back at their house, clearly ignoring Marie's earlier threat. Marie keeps Evan behind her and tells the man that he is not taking Evan anywhere. The man starts talking to Evan directly, telling him they will get away together and leave everything behind. When Marie attacks Evan's father with her knife, he punches her like he punched Evan last time. But this time, he does not lose his balance. As the mother jumps on the father's back trying to stop him, he throws her at the wall, which disorientates her. He grabs a thick stick and starts hitting the woman with all his might. Evan looks helpless and shocked watching the senseless violence unfolding in front of him. As Evan's father makes sure that Marie is subdued, he approaches Evan calmly and promises two things: not to hurt him ever again; and everything will be ok. Seeing his mother beaten senseless by a man who already punched him before is enough for Evan to make a decision. He stabs his father in the chest with his mother's knife, then slits the man's throat with unflinching precision. Marie watches this scene still crying on the floor. Then she goes and buries the body in their garden while Evan watches her with an emotionless face covered in blood. Marie holds Evan in her arms again, starts caressing his back, gently telling him that he is a good boy, and everything will be alright. Evan is not weeping this time. He probably will never cry again.

Depicting the causes and consequences of domestic violence so vividly and undauntedly makes *Bloodline* a difficult film to watch. Its provocative perspective on family traumas, abusive fathers, and how they can create a murderer who kills other abusive men in order to protect vulnerable teenagers makes the moral basis of the narrative even murkier. With an unblinking and fearless attitude, similar to the story of Lisbeth Salander in Chapter 4, the story deliberately forces the viewer to understand, and in some parts empathise with Evan whose inner traumatised child has never recovered and is re-living the same trauma over and over again every time he abducts an abusive father. His three murder scenes with Ray's shamelessly neo-Nazi father Louis (Nick Boraine), Kelly's impenitently perverse uncle Frederick (Dusty Sorg), and Chris's drug addict (and manipulative) father Mark (Leith M. Burke) specifically highlight the story's controversial position: some people might argue that this serial killer is doing a favour to society as he is swiftly getting rid of racists, rapists, and junkies. However, the director is also delving deep into the psychology of crime and criminals through the character of Evan, showing the unhealed wound, the core of violence in a person who is also the victim of his own father and partially his mother.

Different scholars looked at the history of violence and crime, and tried to answer very basic questions: what are the characteristics of a criminal? How does one commit a crime? Why do they do it? Who is the victim? Why and how does criminality go up in societies at different time periods (Gurr, 1981; Sindall, 1990; King, 1996)? Theories on the biological roots of crime, especially in American culture linked violent acts with (mainly young and single) men, arguing that the aggression is down to genetic make-up (Courtwright, 1996). Roth (2009, 2011), on the other hand, noted that violence can find itself a breeding ground in recurrent and persistent personal experiences of being ridiculed, treated with contempt, abused, neglected, excluded, or simply rejected. These experiences have the power to create deep psychological wounds which can transform calm and peaceful people into violent criminals over time. Using thousands of court records on rape and homicide, Wiener's

(2004) study of manliness and crime in Victorian England also highlighted the discussion of gender dynamics in the history of violence and victimisation, looking at both homicidal women and homicidal men.

The World Health Organization's Mental Health Survey (Kessler et al., 2017), a study which looked at the prevalence of trauma exposure in 26 countries (including both lower and higher income countries such as Nigeria and New Zealand), found that, based on over 70,000 respondents and more than 25 types of traumatic events (such as interpersonal violence, war, or accidents), the global exposure rate was 70.4 per cent. These findings support previous results of other studies where scholars have argued that around 70–90 per cent of individuals would experience a traumatic event during their lifetimes (Resnick et al., 1993; Breslau, 2009). It is also known that experiencing highly emotional and stressful events can directly affect the memory and cognitive functioning of individuals, including their psychological regulation of these traumatic experiences after the actual event (Blanchette and Giroux, 2021). While these studies help us understand the nature of the human mind, how it is affected by traumatic events, the reasons why some people become criminals after such an event remain a mystery.

Bloodline, through its morbid take on fatherhood and trauma, presents two contentious questions: for the greater good, is it ethical to kill a person who is unrepentant and is nothing but a source of abuse; and is it ethical to raise a child with the belief that killing is good? The film explores the answer to the first question by depicting all fathers unfavourably, if not reprehensibly. When Evan's father punches him or beats his mother, there is no shame, remorse, or self-awareness to trigger an expression of regret. He never says 'I am sorry' or takes genuine responsibility for his violent actions. After his drunken punch and scornful abuse, his only attempt is to make Evan believe that his insult was just a casual remark. This rather blasé attitude makes his last promise to Evan even more unconvincing and dishonest, especially right after hurting his mother in front of him.

The other fathers, Louis, Frederick, and Mark, are depicted in a similar fashion. When Evan asks them calmly to describe their feelings and sensations when they abuse their own children/relatives (which appears as a twisted counselling session), the fathers lose their power of speech for a few seconds due to being exposed so transparently. However, they quickly bounce back to their regular entitled attitude. Louis first calls his son a 'faggot', then accuses his kids of pushing him to a point of no return where he reacts violently, a classic case of victim blaming. Frederick chooses the same route and argues that 'it is not rape if the girl/woman wants it', describing his niece as a piece of meat. Mark, on the other hand, tries to manipulate Evan by using addiction recovery programme slogans, arguing that he relapses into drug-taking and violence because it is a part of his recovery. Evan does not buy it and forces him to face his denial, that he truly enjoys getting high and he does not care about his son. Evan tells

Mark specifically that all Chris wants is his father to love him, something every child needs and deserves, something Mark has never done and will never do. Hearing this, Mark turns spiteful and calls Evan a monster, unable to be a real father or a husband. As the irony of that last remark is lost on Mark, the final sensations he feels are the warmth of Evan's hand on his shoulder and the coldness of the sharp metal cutting his throat.

For the second question, the film deliberately pursues a narrative where mothers are depicted as having the same capacity for violence as fathers. Especially through the character of Marie, a domestic violence victim, the director turns a mother into a criminal in the name of 'protecting the family'.[2] As she buries the body of her husband, her words to her traumatised son are chilling. Without hesitation, she tells Evan that he is a good boy. After all, Evan did protect himself and his mother from a threatening man. But by associating a murder his son has just committed with goodness, she not only influences Evan's judgement and ethical principles but also paves the way for him to justify his future crimes. This justification is especially visible in his last counselling session with Chris who is grieving (62:22). Evan, straight after killing Mark, explains to Chris that Mark's death can be a blessing in disguise because he will not be coming back to beat Chris or his mother. Coming from experience, he says that some men never change, and they are unable to feel remorse for their horrible behaviour.

So, is Evan a psychotic criminal due to his lack of guilt? Or is he still a child in a grown man's body, re-creating the same experience he had with his father, hopelessly expecting other abusive fathers to show a shred of shame and regret? In this gruesome tale of fatherhood, it appears that Evan is actu-ally the pale criminal Costello (2002) is referring to. He is forever trapped in pain and yearning to be understood. He tries to compartmentalise his life: the goodness, the care, and his love for children (including his own) is retained in the social worker/father persona who works during the sunny days of LA. After sunset, the darkness sets in and his serial killer persona emerges, stop-ping other fathers who hurt their children like he stopped his own father. Being a creature of both light and darkness, he tries to exorcise the pain his father inflicted on him by punching and stabbing other men who act and talk exactly like his father.

Even though Evan's soul is pining for paternal love, the love his father never showed him, he is full of paternal love himself. When he holds his newborn son in his arms (13:11), he promises the little baby four things: not to hurt him; not to judge him; not to leave him; and not to let anything bad happen to him. During his sessions with the students, Evan repeatedly tells them that they should not be feeling guilty for their fathers' behaviour. He regularly reminds them of the fact that they should not feel responsible for the domestic horrors they endure, because they are not at fault. By trying to help and save these children from a lifetime of self-reproach, by listening to their pain with unconditional positive regard, by being the caring and understanding male figure in their lives without judging, hurting, or disrespecting them, Evan becomes a grey mentor to them. Walking a murky path of criminality and compassion, he dwells in the shadows of fatherhood.

The film ends with him and Lauren holding their baby. As murderers, they have successfully hidden their crimes. As parents, they have successfully protected their family. Therefore, they look peaceful, with a certain sense of happiness. With that shot, the film invites the viewers to discuss if this is the definition of a happy family. In *Bloodline*'s universe, it seems that domestic happiness is possible when a father satisfies his need for violence (and/or justice) elsewhere, when he embraces his shadow away from his own home. However, the nature and the scope of that happiness is open to debate.

Red, grey, and others: bits and pieces of wisdom

Colour, by definition, is the personal and subjective experience/sensation, forever associated with and connected to light (Reber et al., 2009). It is experienced by most human beings, and therefore its symbolism is regarded as universal. Used in astronomy, psychology, and even in religious contexts, colours contain and convey information which people immediately perceive and interpret accordingly. Varying with cultural environments, historical perspectives, intentions and aspirations, colours continue to make ideas, impressions, and feelings known and understandable. As Ronnberg and Martin (2010a) note, colours communicate temperament and temperature, feelings and values, class and hierarchy, contrasts and tensions, the nature of matter and its phases during its journey through many transmutations.

In *The Accountant* and *Bloodline* two colours repeatedly appear: red; and grey. As complex characters both trying to survive and protect other people, neither Christian nor Evan hesitate to kill. While their scenes of murder – as well as their motives and methods – are completely different, they include the same internal bodily fluid spattered or splashed across the screen. Even though Christian is extremely efficient in hand-to-hand combat, as an extension of his laser-sharp focus and swiftness, he prefers to finish any and every conflict with a gun. Evan, on the other hand, specifically uses a sharp knife to kill in a violent way – but only after the abusive fathers he abducted refuse to show any genuine remorse. In both films, on the other hand, not only the blood of the murdered people is visible but also the blood of Christian and Evan as little boys, running down their faces after the punches they take.

The Sun's qualities are represented in blood: fire; heat; and vitality (Chevalier and Gheerbrant, 1996a). As a symbol connected to the Sun, it is inevitably associated with male sky deities, masculinity, nobility, valour, and power. It is the liquid where the mystery of life begins and continues. Because it is considered as the element of divine life flowing through the human body (Biedermann, 1996a), or as the medium of the soul (Chevalier and Gheerbrant, 1996a), shedding blood is forbidden, restricted, or simply considered as taboo. Tied to procreation, it is sometimes referred to as the symbolic basis of shared genetic information and heritage.

Red, on the other hand, is the colour of human blood. As Chevalier and Gheerbrant (1996b) note, there is ambivalence in blood-red – when contained in the body it represents life, and when visible or spilled it represents death. Symbolising the energy of life, passion, libido, sexual energy, aggression, and rage (Ronnberg and Martin, 2010b), it is the colour of Valentine's Day, the planet Mars, and the Roman call to arms. Combining both bravery and cruelty, red and blood are inevitably connected to guns and knives. As explored in Chapter 3, guns are ultimately masculine, penetrating weapons, equally used by criminals and law/justice enforcers. Knives share a similar symbolism due to their phallic shape. Surgery and circumcision, dicing and cooking, stabbing and violence, in other words, several opposites are mingled in this sharp object where life and death, nurturing and killing morph into each other. As another symbol of masculine (and aggressive) penetration, it also symbolises the human intellect (Ronnberg and Martin, 2010c) that pierces through the surface of knowledge, separating the useless and unimportant from useful and meaningful.

Created primarily by the marriage of black and white, grey is the symbolic colour of resurrection in Christianity (Chevalier and Gheerbrant, 1996c), but it is also the symbol for grief, mourning, ashes, all related to low spirits, gloom, shadows, and semi-darkness. However, as Ronnberg and Martin (2010d) point out, different hues of grey can be achieved by mixing any opposite colours – such as green and red, or blue and orange. This makes grey a rather anomalous colour, involving brightness and vividness but all behind a shroud of mysterious darkness. A colour bridging both the aged and the newborns, it not only denotes wisdom (via grey hair/beard), but it is also the first ever colour humans perceive (Chevalier and Gheerbrant, 1996b). This interesting chromatic enigma stands as the perfect symbol for human beings who, as depicted by several belief systems, are products of opposites – male and female, body and soul, good and bad – in a neutral physical form which can change its tonality through choice and wilful action.

These two colours appear repeatedly in both films, highlighting a parallel narrative specifically colour coded for Christian and Evan. Christian's father drives a grey car, teaching his son violence and love – how to kill another person and how to honour family ties. As Christian continues to walk down a meandering path between money laundering and helping law enforcement officials, he also drives a grey vehicle to save Frank, Dolores, and Dana (as well as running away to start a new life). Evan's chosen colour for his vehicle which he uses for his social worker and serial killer activities is, again, grey. While grey is chosen as a background colour for *The Accountant*'s promotional posters where Christian is seen holding a grey semi-automatic shotgun looking away from the camera (which itself is a visual nod to his autism, of which eye-contact avoidance is a known symptom), in *Bloodline*'s posters the background colour is shifting from crimson to dark blue. Evan is directly looking at the camera where half of his face is in the shadows and splattered with blood. Neither Christian nor Evan is smiling.

The contradictions and fluctuations in both red and grey are similar to the synthesis of opposites in Jung's famous archetype, the wise old man. Like Hopcke, Blair (1984) noted that even wise old men can be partly unfavourable, negative, chthonic. In dreams, stories and myths, the wise old man can appear as an authority figure (ibid.), like a magician, doctor, or simply a mentor giving advice to sharpen one's awareness and comprehension in order to assist them in their journey through life (or their current predicament). But then again, if wisdom is a combination of education and experience, learning from adversity, reflecting on it, deriving meaning from it is also a part of that wisdom gained by the mentor and the wisdom shared with the mentee. Symbolically speaking, in a world full of light and darkness, a wise old man is destined to be grey.

In 'Dostoevsky and Parricide', Freud (1928) wrote that if children are brought up without love this can make them delinquent and turn their aggression outward. Jung (CW 10, para. 580), on the other hand, noted that the hunger for power and violence grows when there is an absence of love. Based on human nature, he sees each individual as a part of 'humanity's collective shadow' (ibid, para. 572) and argues that everybody is a potential criminal due to their unavoidable participation in this big cumulative darkness. But instead of tackling it, instead of making determined efforts to confront and have authority over it, people displace their own negative traits or unwanted feelings to other people, animals, objects, or concepts.

Because, for Jung, shadow is, has been, and will continue to be a part of the self as well. Because it can never be separated, and as it is a necessary condition of being whole, one's courage is found where and when they face their shadow. Diligently working to know the qualities of shadow, integrating this unwanted, repressed, hidden parts of personality without being an unconscious slave to them, acknowledging their qualities and mastering them without being controlled by them is an important step towards self-actualisation and individuation. As Benezra (1969) argued, the majority of people wish to find the insight to be fulfilled in life, that necessary wisdom to regulate and harmonise their own nature, the human nature, which is not simply just evil or angelic, but a greater whole than the sum of its parts.[3]

Both the biological offspring of their fathers and the living, breathing result of their fathers' beliefs and actions, Christian and Evan lead a life trying to balance aggression and compassion, legal and criminal, safety and danger, isolation and human connection. Facing an unknown future, they strive in their own ways to reconcile their past with their present. Even though they are fictional characters, their compelling storylines contribute to a bigger discussion of families and fatherhood where every word, said or unsaid, every action (or inaction) of parents ripples in time and leads to consequences. They show that between light and dark, between good and bad, there is a grey area – an area that is inherited, that repeats in each generation. The domain of man, full of shadows.

Notes

1 The mantra 'adapt or die' is also used in the famous action-thriller film *Hanna* (2011) as the most important strategy for survival. Similar to *The Accountant*'s tale of uniquely talented children, this film depicts a young girl whose DNA is secretly and specifically engineered by the CIA in order for her to become a super-soldier. Her father rescues her from this experimental programme when she was a baby, and trains her as a perfect assassin, ready for the day when the CIA returns to either claim her back or kill her.
2 The same narrative applies to Lauren as well. She kills Chris after careful deliberation, and especially after her chat with Marie where she accepts the fact that mothers/women would do anything to protect their children and families. When she tells Chris that it is sad Evan had to kill Mark in order to protect him, she proves that she sees Marie as a kindred spirit.
3 Another interesting duality appears in Jung. A case of similar opposites held together, Jung claimed that he had two personalities – an introvert and an extroverted one. Mentioned in *Memories, Dreams, Reflections* (Jung, 1963) he identified them as Number 1 (day-to-day personality) and Number 2 (primal, more instinctive personality).

References

Discography

Radiohead. (2000) *Kid A.* Parlophone.

Filmography

The Accountant. (2016) Directed by G. O'Connor. USA.
Bloodline. (2018) Directed by H. Jacobson. USA.
Hanna. (2011) Directed by J. Wright. Germany, UK, USA.
Rain Man. (1998) Directed by B. Levinson. USA.

Bibliography

Alaghband-Rad, J., Hajikarim-Hamedani, A. and Motamed, M., (2023) 'Camouflage and masking behavior in adult autism', *Frontiers in Psychiatry*, 14, 1108110. https://doi.org/10.3389/fpsyt.2023.1108110.
American Psychiatric Association. (2022) *Diagnostic and Statistical Manual of Mental Disorders.* 5th ed., text rev. Arlington, VA: American Psychiatric Publishing. https://doi.org/10.1176/appi.books.9780890425787.
Benezra, E. E. (1969) 'Duality of human nature', *The American Journal of Psychiatry*, 125, 1456–1457.
Biedermann, H. (1996a) 'Blood', in *The Wordsworth Dictionary of Symbolism*. Ware: Wordsworth Editions.

Blair, R. L. (1984) 'Archetypal imagery in Max Frisch's *Homo faber*: The Wise Old Man and the Shadow', *The Germanic Review: Literature, Culture, Theory*, 59 (3), 104–108.

Blanchette, I. and Giroux, S. V. (2021) 'Reasoning, trauma, and PTSD: insights into emotion–cognition interaction', in *Psychopathology and Philosophy of Mind*. Abingdon: Routledge, pp. 55–74.

Breslau, N. (2009) 'The epidemiology of trauma, PTSD, and other posttrauma disorders', *Trauma, Violence, and Abuse*, 10(3), 198–210.

Chevalier, J. and Gheerbrant, A. (1996a) 'Blood', in *The Penguin Dictionary of Symbols*. London: Penguin.

Chevalier, J. and Gheerbrant, A. (1996b) 'Red', in *The Penguin Dictionary of Symbols*. London: Penguin.

Chevalier, J. and Gheerbrant, A. (1996c) 'Grey', in *The Penguin Dictionary of Symbols*. London: Penguin.

Cook, J., Hull, L., Crane, L. and Mandy, W., (2021) 'Camouflaging in autism: A systematic review', *Clinical Psychology Review*, 89, 102080. https://doi.org/10.1016/j.cpr.2021.102080.

Costello, S. J. (2002) *The Pale Criminal: Psychoanalytic Perspectives*. New York: Karnac Books.

Courtwright, D. T. (1996) *Violent Land: Single Men and Social Disorder from the Frontier to the Inner City*. Cambridge, MA: Harvard University Press.

Creative Screen Writing. (2019) '"Serial killer has a baby": Henry Jacobson & Avra Fox-Lerner on *Bloodline*', available at: www.creativescreenwriting.com/bloodline/.

First, M.B., *et al.* (2021) 'An organization-and category-level comparison of diagnostic requirements for mental disorders in ICD-11 and DSM-5', *World Psychiatry*, 20(1), 34–51.

Freud, S. (1928) 'Dostoevsky and parricide', in S. Freud, *The Standard Edition of the Complete Psychological Works*, Vol. 21. London: The Hogarth Press.

Gurr, E. (1981) 'Historical trends in violent crime: A critical review of the evidence', *Crime & Justice. An Annual Review of Research*, 3, 295–353.

Harris, T. (1988) *The Silence of the Lambs*. New York: St. Martin's Press.

Harris, T. (1999) *Hannibal*. New York: Delacorte Press.

Hopcke, R. H. (1999) *A Guided Tour of the Collected Works of C. G. Jung*. Boston an: Shambhala Publications.

Joon, P., Kumar, A. and Parle, M. (2021) 'What is autism?', *Pharmacological Reports*, 73(5), 1255–1264. https://doi.org/10.1007/s43440-021-00244-0.

Jung, C. G. (1963) *Memories, Dreams, Reflections*. New York: Pantheon Books.

Jung, C. G. (1970) *The Collected Works of C. G. Jung, Volume 10: Civilization in Transition*. Princeton: Princeton University Press.

Jung, C. G. (1968) *The Collected Works of C. G. Jung, Volume 12: Psychology and Alchemy*. Princeton: Princeton University Press.

Jung, C. G. (1970) *The Collected Works of C. G. Jung, Volume 14: Mysterium Coniunctionis*. Princeton: Princeton University Press.

Jung, C. G. (1977) *The Collected Works of C. G. Jung, Volume 18: The Symbolic Life*. Princeton: Princeton University Press.

Kessler, R. C., *et al.* (2017) 'Trauma and PTSD in the WHO world mental health surveys', *European Journal of Psychotraumatology*, 8(sup5), 1353383. https://doi.org/10.1080/20008198.2017.1353383.

King, P. (1996) 'Punishing assault: The transformation of attitudes in the English courts', *Journal of Interdisciplinary History*, 27(1), 43–74.

Lindsay, J. (2005) *Darkly Dreaming Dexter*. New York: Knopf Doubleday.

Livingston, L.A., Shah, P. and Happé, F., (2019) 'Compensatory strategies below the behavioural surface in autism: A qualitative study', *The Lancet Psychiatry*, 6(9), 766–777.

McGrew, S. (2019) 'Interview: Director/co-writer Henry Jacobson for Bloodline', available at: www.nightmarishconjurings.com/2019/09/26/interview-director-co-w riter-henry-jacobson-for-bloodline/.

Reber, A. S., Allen, R., and Reber, E. S. (2009) 'Colour', in *Penguin Dictionary of Psychology*. London: Penguin Books.

Resnick, H. S., Kilpatrick, D. G., Dansky, B. S., Saunders, B. E., & Best, C. L. (1993) 'Prevalence of civilian trauma and posttraumatic stress disorder in a representative national sample of women', *Journal of Consulting and Clinical Psychology*, 61(6), 984–991.

Ronnberg, A. and Martin, K. (eds) (2010a) 'Color', in *The Book of Symbols: Reflections on Archetypal Images*. Cologne: Taschen.

Ronnberg, A. and Martin, K. (eds) (2010b) 'Red', in *The Book of Symbols: Reflections on Archetypal Images*. Cologne: Taschen.

Ronnberg, A. and Martin, K. (eds) (2010c) 'Knife/dagger', in *The Book of Symbols: Reflections on Archetypal Images*. Cologne: Taschen.

Ronnberg, A. and Martin, K. (eds) (2010d) 'Gray', in *The Book of Symbols: Reflections on Archetypal Images*. Cologne: Taschen.

Roth, R. (2009) *American Homicide*. Cambridge, MA: Harvard University Press.

Roth, R. (2011) 'Biology and the deep history of homicide', *British Journal of Criminology*, 51, 535–555.

Sindall, R. (1990) *Street Violence in the Nineteenth Century: Media Panic or Real Danger?*Leicester: Leicester University Press.

Yu, Y., Ozonoff, S., and Miller, M. (2024) 'Assessment of Autism Spectrum Disorder', *Assessment*, 31(1), 24–41. https://doi.org/10.1177/10731911231173089.

Wiener, M. (2004) *Men of Blood: Violence, Manliness and Criminal Justice in Victorian England*. Cambridge: Cambridge University Press.

World Health Organization. (2019) *International Statistical Classification of Diseases and Related Health Problems*. 11th ed. Geneva: World Health Organization. Available at: https://icd.who.int.

Chapter 6

Quo vadis?

Where are you going?

Leaving the religious context in the New Testament from which this Latin phrase originates aside, *quo vadis* is an idiomatic expression used today to understand one's set of circumstances and their direction of travel. Prompting the examination and the awareness of one's own mental and emotional processes, the question 'where are you going?' calls for an answer about one's wishes, desires, intentions, and what they are planning to do about them. It is an invite for self-reflection, a momentary pause to assess the past, present and the future, all tied together and becoming apparent through decisions, actions, and their consequences. It is a question, yes. But it is also a reminder for people to be mindful of their bearings, orientation, and conduct on their journey of personal change and development.

Men, masculinities, and fatherhood have been under close academic inspection for many years. Especially after the arrival of the thought-provoking interdisciplinary survey *Handbook of Studies on Men and Masculinities* (Kimmel et al., 2005), which covered gender dynamics and the geographical, religious, political, financial, and sexual ties that bind men and women, an even faster changing world and shifting topography continue to bring new perspectives and questions about men and fathers. From fears of ecological collapse fuelled by notions of destructively dominant masculinities (Hultman and Pulé, 2020) to queer family relations and new definitions of kinship (Goodfellow, 2015), from German neo-fascist youth (Hörschelmann, 2005) to asking if masculinity is now an outdated concept (Tosh, 2011), from discussing sports through its relation to male identities (Kidd, 2013) to questioning the male dominance both in monogamy and plural marriages (Schippers, 2018), research in social sciences and humanities is still growing, discovering new talking points and contexts. With the arrival of smart home technologies and AI powered devices, male dominance and masculinity in software engineering has also become a hot topic, and is discussed in academia (Pink et al., 2022).

Media studies' engagement with this subject has shown a similar growth. For example, Salter and Blodgett (2017) look at the nature of 'hero' concept in science fiction and fantasy media targeting geek culture and this culture's hostility

DOI: 10.4324/9781003394488-6

towards women. Smith et al. (2018) investigate a broad range of sexualities and their representation in media, including the metrosexual man, BDSM-based relationships, and how disability can be perceived as monstrosity or freakishness. While Clark (2013) looks at the connections between digital media and parenting from apps to traps, Thompson (2023) investigates how patriarchal dominance presented in a series of Tom Hanks films. Films such as *Transamerica* (2005) and *Cowboys* (2020), TV shows such as *Transparent* (2014) and *The Fosters* (2013) continue to shape both academic and non-academic discussions on the definitions of parenthood, family, gender, and masculinity.

So, the question remains. After all this analysis, investigation, dissection, even politically charged point-scoring, where is this discussion on men going? Better yet, where are fathers going? Hearn (2002) noted that fathers/fatherhood represent a historically constructed power, an institution. If that is true, and if today people are searching for a powerful/dominant figure while deconstructing, dismantling that power/institution/dominance at the same time, what would fathers do? What would they choose? Myths repeatedly tell us that even tyrant gods are removed from power. If even gods cannot stop being overthrown, what would happen to mortal man? Will man hold on to power, relentlessly, hopelessly, in eternally repeating cycles?

Hollis (1994) asked individuals to oppose anyone who says one becomes a man (or more masculine) when they exercise power over another – regardless of age or gender. He wrote that the most crucial change – a revolution – would begin at home when men decide to be honest with themselves and their children about the meaning and nature of power – that true power is not singular, myopic, or selfish. It is dynamic and plural. A balance between opposites, it empowers others as much as it empowers oneself (Arrien, 1991). Then maybe, when fathers ask themselves where they are going, when they practise the true nature of power, when they put effort into facing and controlling their shadow, maybe their children will not be lost, they will not be harmed.

Until then … keep asking.

References

Filmography

Cowboys. (2020) Directed by A. Kerrigan. USA.
Transamerica. (2005) Directed by D. Tucker. USA.

TV series

The Fosters. (2013) ABC/Freeform, 3 June. Available at: www.freeform.com/shows/the-fosters.
Transparent. (2014) Amazon Studios, 6 February. Available at: www.amazon.com/Transparent-Season-1/dp/B089XSMKR4.

Bibliography

Arrien, A. (1991) *The Tarot Handbook: Practical Applications of Ancient Visual Symbols*. London: The Aquarian Press.

Clark, L. S. (2013) *The Parent App: Understanding Families in the Digital Age*. Oxford: Oxford University Press.

Goodfellow, A. (2015) *Gay Fathers, Their Children, and the Making of Kinship*. New York: Fordham University Press.

Hearn, J. (2002) 'Men, fathers, and the state: national and global relations', in B. Hobson (ed.) *Making Men into Fathers: Men, Masculinities and the Social Politics of Fatherhood*. Cambridge: Cambridge University Press, pp. 245–272.

Hollis, J. (1994) *Under Saturn's Shadow: The Wounding and Healing of Men*. Toronto: Inner City Books.

Hörschelmann, K. (2005) 'Deviant masculinities: representations of neo-fascist youth in eastern Germany', in B. van Hoven and K. Hörschelmann (eds) *Spaces of Masculinities: Critical Geographies*. New York: Routledge, pp. 138–152.

Hultman, M. and Pulé, P. (2020) 'Ecological masculinities: a response to the Manthropocene question?', in L. Gottzén, U. Mellström, and T. Shefer (eds) *Routledge International Handbook of Masculinity Studies*. New York: Routledge, pp. 477–487.

Kidd, B. (2013) 'Sports and masculinity', *Sport in Society*, 16(4), 553–564.

Kimmel, M., Hearn, J. and Connell, R. W. (2005) *Handbook of Studies on Men and Masculinities*. Thousand Oaks: Sage.

Pink, S., Strengers, Y., Martin, R. and Dahlgren, K. (2022) 'Smart home masculinities', *Australian Feminist Studies*, 37(112), 117–133. https://doi.org/10.1080/08164649.2023.2197155.

Salter, A. and Blodgett, B. (2017) *Toxic Geek Masculinity in Media: Sexism, Trolling, and Identity Policing*. New York: Springer International Publishing.

Schippers, M. (2018) 'The monogamous couple, gender hegemony, and polyamory', in J. W. Messerschmidt, M. A. Messner, R. Connell, P. Y. Martin (eds) *Gender Reckonings: New Social Theory and Research*. New York: New York University Press, pp. 314–330.

Smith, C., Attwood, F. and McNair, B. (2018) *The Routledge Companion to Media, Sex and Sexuality*. Abingdon: Routledge.

Thompson, B. E. (2023) 'What Are You Crying For? Renegotiating White Masculine Hegemony through Melodramatic Excess in the 1990s Films of Tom Hanks.' Doctoral dissertation, Chapman University.

Tosh, J. (2011) 'The history of masculinity: An outdated concept?', in J. H. Arnold and S. Brady (eds) *What is Masculinity? Genders and Sexualities in History*. London: Palgrave Macmillan, pp. 17–34.

Index

abandonment xxii, 17n2, 43; *see also* neglect

Abraham, Nicholas 12

abuse: as reason for adolescent offence 72; child financial abuse 43; child physical abuse 42; child sexual abuse 42–43; definition of 41–42; emotional abuse 43; ill effects of 44, 51, 53; psychological maltreatment 52–53; system abuse 43; *see also* neglect

Accountant, The: balancing light and dark 100; blood symbolism 98; grey symbolism 99; gun symbolism 99; knife symbolism 99; plot summary 88–89 red symbolism 99; resilience 92; shadow 100; wise old man symbolism 100; *see also* autism

Ad Astra: Apollo 1 plaque 3; door symbolism 4; dysfunctional father-son relationship 1; rejection of human connection 8; hero's journey structure 1; internal and external journey 4; failed marriage 14; Mars symbolism 7; Neptune symbolism 8; monkey symbolism 6; monomyth 1; narcissism 10, 12; suicide 13, 16; the Moon symbolism 5; vehicle symbolism 5; *see also* neglect adverse childhood experiences 9, 43; *see also* neglect

Anderson, Paul Thomas 44, 45, 59n6, n7, n8, n13; see also *Magnolia*

Anthony, Susan B. xv

Ares 7, 16; *see also Ad Astra*; Mars

Arrien, Angeles 105

Asperger's 89

atheism as a result of abuse 44; *see also* abuse

attachment theory xix–xx

autism 89–90

Balcom, Dennis A. 12

Blackwood, Algernon 4

Bloodline: abusive father examples 95, 96–97; blood symbolism 98; connection between absence of love and violence 100; Dexter Morgan 93; domestic violence scenes 94–95; grey symbolism 99; Hannibal Lecter 93; knife symbolism 99; maternal influence on serial killer ethics 97; plot summary 93–94; psychological roots of violent criminality 95; qualities of the Sun 98; red symbolism 99; serial killer as grey mentor 97–98; *see also* abuse; pale criminal

Bodichon, Barbara Leigh Smith xv

Boogie Nights 44

Bowlby, John xix

captain archetype, the xxi

Campbell, Joseph 1

Case 39 65

child abuse: definition of 42; research issues 43; *see also* abuse

childhood exposure to domestic violence as a form of child abuse 43

Cell, The 41

Clarke, Arthur Charles 16

conformity to masculinity norms inventory-94 xiv

Contact (Sagan) 17, 17n5

Corneau, Guy xxi, 16

Costello, Stephen J. 92–93, 97

Cousineau, Phil 1

Cowboys 105

relation to life cycles 4; *see also* wise old man
wise old man: as archetype 85, 100; *see also Accountant, The*; educator archetype, the
Wolff, Tobias Jonathan Ansell: 48, 51; see also *This Boy's Life*

yang xiii, 13, 16, 56

yin 5, 16, 56

Zeus: Athena's birth 70; ending his father's rule 65, 77, 81n1; linguistic connection xi; punishment of Prometheus 27; symbol of archetypal and intergenerational struggle 36
Zoloft 90

For Product Safety Concerns and Information please contact our EU
representative GPSR@taylorandfrancis.com
Taylor & Francis Verlag GmbH, Kaufingerstraße 24, 80331 München, Germany